T0318476

Cambridge Elements ≡

Elements in Business Strategy
edited by
J.-C. Spender
Kozminski University

EFFECTUATION

Rethinking fundamental concepts in the social sciences

Saras Sarasvathy
University of Virginia

CAMBRIDGE
UNIVERSITY PRESS

Shaftesbury Road, Cambridge CB2 8EA, United Kingdom

One Liberty Plaza, 20th Floor, New York, NY 10006, USA

477 Williamstown Road, Port Melbourne, VIC 3207, Australia

314–321, 3rd Floor, Plot 3, Splendor Forum, Jasola District Centre,
New Delhi – 110025, India

103 Penang Road, #05-06/07, Visioncrest Commercial, Singapore 238467

Cambridge University Press is part of Cambridge University Press & Assessment,
a department of the University of Cambridge.

We share the University's mission to contribute to society through the pursuit of
education, learning and research at the highest international levels of excellence.

www.cambridge.org
Information on this title: www.cambridge.org/9781009475754

DOI: 10.1017/9781009103985

First published 2024

A catalogue record for this publication is available from the British Library.

ISBN 978-1-009-47575-4 Hardback
ISBN 978-1-009-10835-5 Paperback
ISSN 2515-0693 (online)
ISSN 2515-0685 (print)

Cambridge University Press & Assessment has no responsibility for the persistence
or accuracy of URLs for external or third-party internet websites referred to in this
publication and does not guarantee that any content on such websites is, or will
remain, accurate or appropriate.

Effectuation

Rethinking fundamental concepts in the social sciences

Elements in Business Strategy

DOI: 10.1017/9781009103985
First published online: May 2024

Saras Sarasvathy
University of Virginia

Author for correspondence: Saras Sarasvathy, saras@virginia.edu

Abstract: Effectuation has become the basis for educating entrepreneurs and managers. Derived from cognitive and behavioral economic studies of expert entrepreneurs, effectuation shows how to cocreate value in highly uncertain situations. The framework of effectuation consists in techniques that minimize the use of predictive information and ways to turn control itself into strategy. In doing so, the effectual process opens up radically new ways to rethink a variety of fundamental concepts in all the social sciences. This ranges from risk and return to markets and governments in economics; attitudes toward ends and means in psychology; opportunism and altruism in social psychology; and even success and failure in strategic management. Effectuation theory inverts several older approaches in what Herbert Simon referred to as the "sciences of the artificial." These inversions suggest an entrepreneurial method based on non-predictive control that complements the predictive control techniques of the scientific method.

Keywords: entrepreneurship, behavioral economics, expertise, innovation, uncertainty

ISBNs: 9781009475754 (HB), 9781009108355 (PB), 9781009103985 (OC)
ISSNs: 2515-0693 (online), 2515-0685 (print)

Contents

What experts think matters far less than *how* they think. If we want realistic odds on what will happen next, coupled with a willingness to admit mistakes, we are better off turning to experts who embody the intellectual traits of Isaiah Berlin's prototypical fox—those who "know many little things," draw from an eclectic array of traditions, and accept ambiguity and contradiction as inevitable features of life—than we are turning to Berlin's hedgehogs—those who "know one big thing," toil devotedly within one tradition, and reach for formulaic solutions to ill-defined problems.

Philip Tetlock

Political Judgment: How Good Is It? How Can We Know?

(Tetlock, 2009, p. 2)

1 Origins in Entrepreneurial Expertise

The name effectuation denotes the idea that we can view causes and effects from opposite directions. We can start with an effect and examine causes leading up to it. Or we can begin with causes and consider effects that can ensue from them. Note that the latter already is a pluralistic view of reality.

My own experiences as an entrepreneur led to the undertaking of the academic research that resulted in the theory, logic, and worldview of effectuation. Over the past two decades, that research has grown into a stream of hundreds of journal articles, as well as a variety of teaching materials developed by educators around the world. This Element takes effectuation to the next stage by spelling out implications for practical entrepreneurs within and outside large organizations. It offers frameworks for building ventures, markets, opportunities, and even the very environments and worlds within which these live and thrive.

Surprisingly, it turns out that the effectual process is also a process for figuring out what is worth building in the first place.

In this Element, I will tell the story of how the idea came to be, summarize what has been done with it so far, and then explore how it transforms several fundamental concepts we take for granted in the social sciences. I present each of these transformations visually. In each case, the effectual tends to precede one or more concepts currently being taken for granted in extant paradigms.

In terms of writing style, although I try to use minimalistic third-person language throughout most of the Element, the use of the first person in some places made the writing easier. I hope it also makes the reading easier.

1.1 Effectuation: The Original Study of Expert Entrepreneurs

The theory, or more accurately the logic of effectuation, originated in a study of entrepreneurial expertise (Sarasvathy, 2009). In conversation with Herbert Simon, advisor to my doctoral dissertation, I designed a think-aloud protocol study of expert entrepreneurs. Drawing upon studies of expertise in over 200 domains, I defined an expert entrepreneur as someone with ten or more years of full-time immersive experience starting and running multiple ventures, including successes and failures, and at least one public company. The objective for the sampling frame was to ensure breadth and depth of experience, as well as proven verifiable performance. A total of 245 people fit the criteria, and I wrote to all of them, of whom 45 accepted. The final sample encompassed a wide variety of industries, ranging from software and biotech to retail, personal services, even railroad and steel.

The research design used the classic think-aloud method from expertise studies (Ericsson & Simon, 1993). In this method, experts are asked to do what they typically do in their domain of expertise while concurrently thinking aloud continuously. For example, chess grand masters would be asked to play chess but continuously think aloud as they contemplated their next move. Concurrent thinking aloud accomplishes two things. First, it prevents people from making up stories retrospectively, whether about how or why they make the moves they do. Second, it allows the researcher to reconstruct step-by-step the heuristics or rules of thumb used by the experts. The term heuristics here refers to how experts process information during the task: which pieces of information they ignore, which ones they pay attention to and in what order, how they combine bits with other bits and/or transform them in which ways, and so on (Kuusela & Paul, 2000).

For my study of expert entrepreneurs, I created a seventeen-page problem set of ten typical decisions that all entrepreneurs are confronted with in starting and running new ventures. By design, the experts in my sample had very little in common in terms of industry or technology experience. Yet, they had almost everything in common in terms of entrepreneurial experience. Therefore, I made entrepreneurship itself the product for the problem set used in the think-aloud task in the study. Remember, the "task" consisted of building a venture.

The seventeen-page problem set began with a brief description of the idea for a new venture based on an educational game of entrepreneurship, followed by a series of questions about potential customers, competitors, and growth prospects. I also asked what information the subjects would seek about these and how they would go about obtaining that information. I then provided information I had gathered about this venture idea and asked them to make a series of decisions, including marketing, funding, hiring, growth, crisis management, and exit.

I went out in person to each subject to gather and record the think-aloud data. Subjects spent anywhere between two and four hours on the task. During the task, I would not interrupt or ask questions, except to prompt them to continue thinking aloud if they paused for more than four seconds. After they completed the think-aloud task, I would ask a few open-ended interview questions.

Even as the recordings were being transcribed, I would listen to the protocols over and over again in airports, planes, and hotels, and in between travel times. Initially, the recordings sounded like any entrepreneur anywhere talking about building new ventures. But listening closely and repeatedly, one thing started emerging from the data, almost by the third protocol. Each expert entrepreneur expressed negative opinions about doing market research. Comments ranged from, "I don't believe in market research" to "I would not do anything like surveys or focus groups because they have never worked for me."

As I puzzled over why they might be averse to market research and how they made marketing decisions while ignoring market research data, I eventually discovered that their comments generalized beyond market research to encompass all predictive information.

Bottom line was that expert entrepreneurs exhibited a deep distrust of predictive information of any kind. In follow-on interviews, one subject put it this way: "I think predictions about the past are OK. But don't believe anyone who is predicting the future, even when they are talking about what they themselves will or won't do or want or don't want."

Armed with this insight, I set about scouring a variety of literatures on prediction. One of the earliest and most inspiring insights on the topic came from Frank Knight's (1921) dissertation, "Risk, Uncertainty and Profit," which was and is still in print and studied to this day. To analyze the think-aloud data, I devised a coding scheme based on Frank Knight's distinctions between risk, uncertainty, and true unknowability (what we call Knightian uncertainty).

1. Risk refers to situations characterized by a known distribution but an unknown draw. Trying to guess the color of a ball drawn from an urn containing fifty green balls and fifty red balls is an example of risk.
2. Uncertainty consists of unknown draws from unknown distributions. This is akin to guessing the color of a ball drawn from an urn consisting of an unknown number of balls of an unknown number of colors. Here, we would have to make repeated draws over time to create an estimation of the distribution of balls in the urn. Thereafter, we can do calculations of odds, similar to those in the case of risk.
3. Knightian uncertainty comprises situations where the distribution is not only unknown but also unknowable. We can imagine this to be an urn that consists of totally random objects, not just balls. No matter how many draws we make from it, we will not be any closer to an accurate estimation of what is in the urn.

It turned out that the lessons that expert entrepreneurs had learned through years of deliberate practice, starting and running ventures, had taught them ways to tackle this third kind of fundamental unpredictability (Dew et al., 2018; Ericsson, Krampe, & Tesch-Römer, 1993). Additionally, they also learned to deal with ambiguities about their own goals (March, 1978; Slovic, 1995) as well as ways to determine what would count as relevant and irrelevant information in the face of unknowable futures combined with ambiguous goals (Chiappe & Kukla, 1996; Fodor, 1983/2008).

In sum, the following three aspects characterize the effectual problem space:

1. Knightian uncertainty: The future is not only unknown, but also unknowable
2. Goal ambiguity: Goals are often not clearly specified, even when aspirations are present
3. Isotropy: It is not obvious which information is relevant and which is not

Note that the term "isotropy" has slightly different meanings in different contexts. In engineering, for example, it refers to the property of a material that is invariant with respect to direction. In philosophy, it refers to the epistemic interconnectedness of beliefs in the sense that "Crudely, everything that the scientist knows is, in principle, relevant to determining what else he ought to believe. In principle, our botany constrains our astronomy, if only we could think of ways to make them connect" (Fodor, 2008, p. 903). Cognitively speaking, " . . . isotropy is the principle that *any* fact may turn out to be (ir)relevant to the confirmation of any other" (Fodor, 2008, p. 905). In other words, isotropy points to the problem of informational relevance.

1.2 Effectuation: Developments Over the Past Two Decades

Over the past two decades, I have developed the findings from that first study into the five principles of effectuation that three of my coauthors and I explored empirically and enhanced theoretically (Sarasvathy, 2001; Sarasvathy, 2009). Nicholas Dew studied effectuation through an in-depth history of the radio frequency identification industry, which led to the development of the dynamic process model in Figure 1 (Sarasvathy & Dew, 2005). Robert Wiltbank collected data from angel investors to help develop performance implications for effectuation (Wiltbank et al., 2009). And Stuart Read has worked to connect both principles and process to the practice of marketing, entrepreneurial pedagogy, and strategy inside large corporations, as well as within small and new ventures (Read et al., 2009; Read et al., 2016; Read, Song, & Smit, 2009). Together, the four of us developed the first survey-based measures and published over a dozen peer-reviewed articles using a variety of different methods.

After the first few of our articles appeared, more researchers became interested, and now over 700 articles have been published, including about 100 in top-ranked journals (Alsos et al., 2019). However, most of the important work remains to be

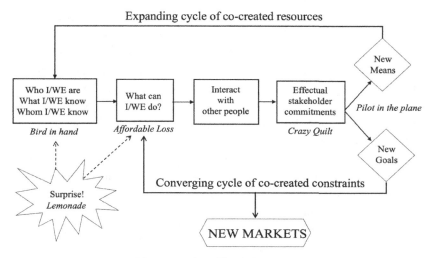

Figure 1 The effectual process

done. Extant works have largely focused on demonstrating existence. These studies found evidence for the use of effectuation in several different business domains, such as family business (Bloemen-Bekx, Lambrechts, & Van Gils, 2021), international business (Harms & Schiele, 2012; Karami, Wooliscroft, & McNeill, 2020; Mainela & Puhakka, 2009), social enterprise (Corner & Ho, 2010; Servantie & Rispal, 2018), R&D departments (Brettel et al., 2012; Fischer et al., 2021; Szambelan & Jiang, 2020) and social media (Fischer & Reuber, 2011). Data have been gathered from over fifty countries using a variety of methods ranging from surveys and case studies to mathematical models and conjoint analyses. Several studies have also examined the relationship between differential or combinatorial uses of predictive and effectual approaches in these different settings, relating them to different types of entrepreneurial and innovative activities (Alsos et al., 2016; Frese, Geiger, & Dost, 2020; Gabrielsson & Politis, 2011; Reymen et al., 2017; Smolka et al., 2018).

However, as I will outline in this Element, in-depth examinations of the radical revisions of fundamental concepts in the social sciences that the logic of effectuation calls for have barely begun to be touched upon. Before I get to that in Section 2 of this Element, let me provide a brief outline of the principles, process, and performance implications of effectuation.

1.3 Effectuation: Principles, Process, and Performance Implications

The original study yielded five heuristics. At first glance, these could be seen as unconnected, but a deeper look shows that they are logically consistent with each other. Each reduces, and even minimizes, the use of predictive information. Each also offers systematic criteria for acting in the face of a truly unknowable future. Together, they form a logic of non-predictive control.

This might come as a surprise to those imbued with the notion that prediction and control are tightly related, even inseparable. In other words, either prediction is already equal to control, or any distance between them is purely a matter of missing information. Both of these conceptions rule out the possibility of prediction being orthogonal to control.

Traditionally, the relationship between prediction and control has been dominated by the positivist paradigm in science, where control is impossible without prediction. In this view, there is a congruence between prediction and control (Sellars, 1939). Even in situations where we do not have access to predictive information in full, or where there exists some distance between prediction and control, it is still prediction that leads to control. In other words, we need predictive information and strategies based on that to achieve control. A simple example may serve to clarify these relationships between prediction and control. Predicting whether it will rain or not can help us avoid getting wet. Moreover, accurate predictions of rain can help us decide whether we need to carry an umbrella or even choose whether to go out at all or not.

However, by simply carrying an umbrella, we can ignore predictions of rain. In this case, by doing something within our control, namely carrying an umbrella, we obviate the need to make predictions, let alone worry about the accuracy of those predictions. It is in this sense that the five heuristics derived from the study of expert entrepreneurs challenge this tight link between prediction and control. Instead, effectuation posits not only distance but also an orthogonal relationship between prediction and control.

In sum, traditional (causal) views are based on the logic: *To the extent we can predict the future, we can achieve control over it.* The effectual view inverts this logic: *To the extent we can work with things within our control, we don't need to predict the future.* Note that both prediction and control can be more or less accurate, more or less error-prone. All the same, the two logics, causal and effectual, point to different sets of possible actions under uncertainty.

In other words, effectuation exposes control itself as a strategy to shape and cocreate new futures. In making new futures, predictions about those futures are neither necessary nor valid. Knowledge about the past and present is still valid and useful, even when such knowledge uses prediction as the touchstone for validity, such as in scientific knowledge. But predictions about what we can and cannot do with such knowledge are often useless and irrelevant. Even more unpredictable are the issues of what other people will and will not do with extant knowledge or how they might react to what we do with it. Yet, people can commit to using things within their control in particular ways that obviate the need to predict what they might otherwise do or not.

Through the actions and interactions of venture building, expert entrepreneurs learn the following five principles of effectuation[1]:

1. **Bird-in-hand:** Instead of clearly defined goals or predicted opportunities, they begin with who they are, what they know, and whom they know.
2. **Affordable loss:** Instead of calculating risk-adjusted expected return for making investments, they invest no more than they can afford to lose.
3. **Crazy quilt:** Instead of targeting particular potential stakeholders for particular resources, they work with anyone and everyone who commits real resources to the venture, allowing those who commit to self-select into the venture as actual stakeholders.
4. **Lemonade:** Instead of avoiding surprises, they leverage both positive and negative contingencies.
5. **Pilot-in-the-plane:** Instead of viewing the future as driven by trends outside their control, they learn how human beings shape and cocreate new possibilities.

The process model in Figure 1 shows how the five principles of effectuaion work together iteratively over time to fabricate a variety of artifacts, including new products, ventures, markets, opportunities, sociopolitical institutions, and other elements of new futures. Note that the process can begin anywhere in the diagram. For ease of comprehension, let us begin with the "bird-in-hand" box.

Effectual entrepreneurs begin with what is already within their control, or more accurately, what they perceive or deem to be within their control. These consist in elements of their identity (who they are), knowledge (what they know), and network (whom they know). Based on means within their control, they come up with possible actions. These actions are usually mundane, even routine parts of the way they live and act, adding up to venture ideas that are not likely brilliant, nor even incrementally innovative.

Note that there is no assumption here that mere possession of something implies any prediction of what one could or should do with it. Any effectuator's knowledge of possible actions based on what they deem within their control may be incomplete or nonexistent, or simply wrong. Yet, by simply taking inventory of what they possess, they can come up with actions they could take, irrespective of whether those actions thereafter lead to any

---

[1] The names of the principles were developed and have evolved over time to make the heuristics more accessible to practitioners and educators. For the purposes of this Element, I will focus more on the intellectual implications for the radical rearrangements of fundamental concepts in Section 2 rather than on the principles themselves.

particular effects they may or may not predict. In other words, there is no need to assume a tight coupling of cause and effect in seeing something as within one's control.

Let's consider again the example of an umbrella. It could be argued that when one sees an umbrella, one sees its predicted effect in protecting us against rain and sun. Yet, when asked what can be done with an umbrella, people come up with a number of other uses for it such as a walking stick, basket, weapon, art, and so on. In the context of a venture, an umbrella could evoke ideas such as insurance (Travelers Insurance), golfing (Arnold Palmer Brands), banking (Citibank), and so on. The point here is that control of means is not limited to one's predictions of effects arising from its use. Instead, simply by approaching means as drivers of actions, it becomes possible to produce a one-to-many mapping from them to a variety of viable and valuable actions, even when the ensuing effects of those actions are not or cannot be predicted.

Effectual entrepreneurs choose between these actions/venture ideas based on what they can afford and are willing to lose. This allows them to keep the downside within their control while allowing upsides to be forged through action rather than predicted ahead of time. Using affordable loss criteria also focuses attention on things worth doing, even if the venture eventually fails. Traversing the first two boxes in Figure 1, consisting of bird-in-hand and affordable loss, can be rather quick, doable on Day 1 as it were. These can also be entirely subjective and idiosyncratic, especially at the beginning of the process.

On Day 2, effectuators start interacting with other people, some of them targeted, but most contingent on their current lives and circumstances. Each interaction offers the possibility of stakeholder self-selection. Parties to each interaction can choose to invest what they can afford to lose, or not.

When an interaction results in commitments from both or all sides, new means start to become available, kick-starting an expanding cycle of resources. At the same time, goals of the new venture also get reshaped, resulting in a converging cycle of constraints. Taken together, the two cycles, expanding and contracting, eventually coagulate into new possibilities.

Along the way, things completely outside the control of all current stakeholders can impact the process, positively or negatively. Effectual stakeholders transform these contingencies into new means and new constraints that keep the process moving forward toward the cocreation of new futures, key elements of which may involve new products, ventures, markets, opportunities, and institutions.

The process does not guarantee success or even completion. Everyone involved always has the option to quit when their affordable loss levels are reached or when an external contingency destroys the venture. However, when success does occur, there is a high probability that the artifact cocreated through that success will be innovative. Similarly, when failure happens, chances are good that its costs would be low since no one loses more than they can afford to lose.

With this succinct summary of effectuation in hand, in Section 2, as we examine its implications for revising a series of taken-for-granted assumptions in the social sciences, we will also delve deeper into the principles and process, as well as flesh out a variety of nuances.

> We have come to think of the actual as one of all possible worlds. We need to repaint that picture. All possible worlds lie within the actual one.
>
> *Nelson Goodman, Fact, Fiction, Forecast* (Goodman, 1983)

2 Effectual Transformations of Fundamental Concepts

It is easy to think that effectuation is the same as not being rational, a deviation from rationality, or simply irrational action. It is important not to fall into such complacency. Instead, we need to confront the fact that an effectual approach quite systematically and radically reverses and rearranges the building blocks of rational and/or conventional models. In this section of the Element, I will examine six pairs of building blocks, with additional sub-blocks in some cases.

Each conceptual building block is illustrated graphically, both in terms of the conventional view and the effectual transformation of that view.

I do not believe the list is complete, yet I will make it as comprehensive as I can in light of the work done till date. We will begin the effort with the rearrangement of the most fundamental conceptual pair: prediction and control.

2.1 Prediction and Control

It is conventional to think of prediction as leading to control. In other words, the better we can predict, the more control we have, at least over our own outcomes, if not over the phenomena themselves. Hark back to the umbrella example earlier. This relationship between prediction and control is depicted as a point on the left-hand side of Figure 2. Contrast this with the right-hand side where this point expands into the two dimensions of a finite space. Another way to see the difference is that in the conventional view, the space between prediction and control vanishes into a dimensionless point.

It is important to note that the prediction-control space is not infinite. Uncertainty bounds the space at any given point in time. Yet, the space can be transformed not only through exogenous forces but also through endogenous actions and interactions, reshaping the uncertainty. In other words, the space itself evolves through time, both through the accumulation of knowledge as in

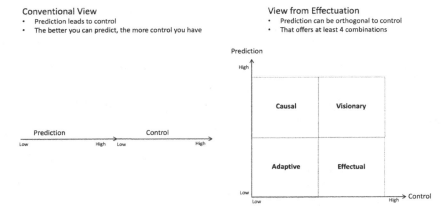

Figure 2 The prediction-control space

science, but also through the cocreation of new ends worth achieving, as in effectual entrepreneurship.

Simply adding the caveat that predictions be empirically testable and falsifiable has led to an astonishing development of knowledge over the course of recent human history. This is why prediction is conventionally considered the cornerstone of science (Feibleman, 1972; Rychlak, 1964). We will delve more into this later in Section 3 when we return to reversed relationships between prediction and control as the core of differentiating the scientific from the entrepreneurial method.

Here, I would like to point out that several developments in business research and education embrace the idea that prediction leads to control. Why do we do market research? So that we can estimate future demand and select between alternate products to cater to it (Bemmaor, 1995). Prediction can help map out the potential market space so we can apply strategic analyses such as Porter's five forces (Porter, 2008) or Strengths Weaknesses Opportunities Threats (Andrews, 1997) to figure out sustainable competitive advantages. In financial decisions, we make estimates of future cash flows and potential risks in order to calculate the net present value (NPV) of risk-adjusted expected returns (Brealey & Myers, 1984). The project with the higher NPV is the optimal candidate for investment. Even in human resources management, we seek to predict which of any two or more candidates is more likely to perform better on the job (Sackett, Gruys, & Ellingson, 1998; Salgado, 2003). And so on.

Business books are replete with ways to predict the future. This can also include predicting the behavior of human beings in the face of predicted and uncertain futures (Harris et al., 2016). Sometimes, these behavioral predictions are inputs into system-level predictions, and at other times, the predicted behaviors indicate outcome scenarios.

Expert entrepreneurs learn the hard way that predictions often don't work, and even when they do, they do not automatically or even easily lead to control. Most times, they do not even tell us how to decide between alternate courses of possible actions, not only in the longer run but also in the immediate future.

Yet, so much of the world is organized around predictive models that potential stakeholders routinely ask for predictions; for example, investors. Most banks require entrepreneurs to calculate and submit financial projections, which in turn rely on predictions of demand and technological trajectories, as well as the future behaviors of actual and potential competitors. Often, macroeconomic forecasts and political trends also feed into these projections. Formal and informal advice related to fundraising urge predictive data collection of one kind or another. Everything from in-depth ethnographic interviews with potential customers (Liedtka, 2014) to big data analyses (Saini, 2018) are offered as tools for building ventures more likely to succeed.

However, these models do not always highlight the fundamental assumptions that they take for granted and build on. For example, what if one is wrong in choosing which people to talk to and gather data from in the first place? What if the current set of possible markets does not include new markets that unexpectedly come to be? Or the biggest assumption of all, namely, that there exists "the" future which can be predicted at all.

Of course, predictive techniques are most useful in the face of risk. When dealing with an unknown draw from a known distribution, we can indeed make accurate predictions that result in better control of outcomes, provided, of course, we have clear preferences on the set of possible outcomes, as in the case of wanting to avoid getting wet in the rain. Prediction can also be useful in the face of unknown draws from unknown distributions. Assuming we have the time and resources to make multiple draws and learn through sophisticated estimation and experimentation techniques, even in the face of uncertainty, better prediction can lead to better outcomes, albeit at a higher cost (namely, the cost of estimation and experimentation).

However, in the face of true or Knightian uncertainty, prediction simply does not and cannot work. Entrepreneurs often face Knightian uncertainty and begin losing faith in prediction. As we will see a little later, they might even overlearn this lesson and choose not to invest in predictive techniques, even when faced with risk and uncertainty, rather than Knightian uncertainty. But they offer reasons as to why they choose to make this error.

In brief, expert entrepreneurs learn the following lesson: *To the extent you are willing to work with things already within your control, you don't need to predict the future.* Nor do you need to chase things outside your control. This allows control to develop into a dimension of its own. One implication of this lesson is that prediction and control can be conceptualized as orthogonal axes, as depicted on the right-hand side of Figure 2. Now, expanding the vanishing point on the left-hand side into a space of four possible strategies for action on the right gives us the CAVE framework:

1. Causal: High in prediction, but low in control (top left)
2. Adaptive: Low in both prediction and control (bottom left)
3. Visionary: High in both prediction and control (top right)
4. Effectual: Low in prediction and high in control (bottom right)

Note that ex ante, these have to do with the perception of what and how much is predictable and/or controllable, not what actually turns out to be so ex post. In other words, expert entrepreneurs learn to perceive the future as unpredictable and rely on things perceived to be within their control as more reliable drivers of what to do next. We will return later to an examination of errors in perceptions as to which quadrant one finds oneself in. For now, let us analyze each of the four quadrants as viable strategies.

The heroic visionary has always been the stuff of legend, intrepidly leading humanity out of caves and on to the conquest of space and time. This is true of entrepreneurship as well. The rags-to-riches myths of Horatio Alger are a case in point (Weiss, 1969). So is the award given to honor perseverance, integrity, and excellence by the Horatio Alger Association of Distinguished Americans. Popular books also celebrate notions of visionaries who can see around the corner, who skate to where the puck will be rather than where it currently is (Christensen, Raynor, & Verlinden, 2001). A similar celebration of vision permeated knowledge development before the scientific method became widely taught (Westfall, 2020). Divine revelation and the ability to "read the signs of nature" were the hallmarks of ability and achievement in the arts and craftsmen's guilds, as opposed to "tinkerers" who chanced upon inventions that, even when useful, could not rise to the theoretical understandings of philosophers and scholastics.

The rise of science arguably eroded the heroic pedestal, slowly replacing it with a more careful and systematic machinery of method. All the same, notions of scientific "genius" continue to spotlight the theoretical accomplishments of men such as Einstein, Turing, and Darwin, while also celebrating the plodding data collection and experimental work of a growing body of thousands of scientists, such as those working on the Hadron Collider or the Human Genome project (Simonton, 1988).

Predictions count not only in the natural sciences but also in the social sciences (Hindman, 2015; Mirowski, 1991). The touchstone for theoretical achievement in any science is the testability of a theory's predictions and the subsequent discoveries arising out of efforts to falsify those predictions. Predictions that stand unfalsified get incorporated into technologies and policies. These rely on the predictions to build useful products and institutions that improve human life and society.

The sciences are careful and cognizant of the fact that predictions do not automatically imply control. In fact, the second half of the twentieth century thoroughly shook up any complacent expectations that scientific knowledge would inevitably lead to complete control of the forces of nature. Developments in quantum physics had already raised doubts that were only reinforced through the mathematics of chaos theory and rising attention to complex and self-organizing phenomena such as weather patterns and viruses (Werndl, 2009). Not to mention the continual contradictions of sociopolitical institutions and the human psyche failing to keep up with technological advances (Gazzaley & Rosen, 2016; Moses, 2007; Volti, 2005).

For now, I call the high prediction-low control (top left) quadrant of Figure 2 "Causal" to signify the fact that predictions offer insights into cause–effect relationships that we can then use to obtain specific effects we seek to obtain.

Given that predictions do not always lead to control and that the increasing speed of technological advances can destabilize markets and societies in unpredictable ways, adaptive approaches remain important in modernity as much, if not more, as in primitive times. Silicon Valley relies on catchphrases such as "agile" and "lean," seeking to shorten the distance between knowledge and action as they both rapidly coevolve to produce novelty and financial value. So much so that the very word "entrepreneurial" is sometimes deemed synonymous with adaptive.

Both causal and adaptive evoke the possibility of sidestepping the unexpected, even when explicitly acknowledging its inexorability. Based on increasingly sophisticated ways to gather and analyze more data, the causal approach assumes that it is possible to carefully plan ways to avoid surprises. The adaptive approach advocates nimbleness. By quickly reacting to incoming surprises, the entrepreneur can both avoid the consequences of unpleasant surprises and jump on new possibilities offered by pleasant ones.

In contrast to these three approaches, effectual entrepreneurs learn systematic ways to minimize the use of prediction. While control is a desirable outcome in all four quadrants, control becomes strategy in the effectual quadrant. This makes sense because prediction is ruled out in the effectual case. Nonpredictive control, also known as effectuation, involves using things within one's control to shape and cocreate rather than predict the future.

2.1.1 Navigating the Four Quadrants of the Prediction-Control Space

In navigating the prediction-control space, novices may not recognize which part of the space they are in, and even when they do, they may not know the appropriate strategies to use. Expert entrepreneurs develop some degree of judgment through experience on both of these issues. All the same, they could still make errors since these spaces themselves change over time. In other words, Type I–II errors can always occur on how predictable or not any given situation may be. In such cases, some form of precommitment to one or the other error forms the only way out. An iconic example of such a precommitment occurs in the justice system (Elster, 2000; Sumner, 1987). While in every case of guilt or innocence, the system seeks to make correct judgments, there will still be cases where even with all the evidence in, it is not clear whether a given defendant is guilty or innocent. In such cases, juries and judges refer to the precommitment of the system to an error – presumption of innocence, in the case of the US. When in doubt, let a guilty person go free rather than incarcerate an innocent person.

Expert entrepreneurs also precommit to an error – when in doubt, treat the future as unpredictable. As one entrepreneur put it

> If you think the future is predictable when it is not, it is likely to prove costly. If you make the mistake of thinking the future is uncertain and it turns out to be predictable, you will quickly learn that. Most importantly, in more predictable situations, people smarter than you and with deeper pockets are likely to get in the game. I prefer not to be in that game. I'm happy to proceed without presuming I can predict anything.

Interestingly, perceiving the future as fundamentally unpredictable and, therefore, seeking to shape it using things already within control can paradoxically result in making predictable futures while concurrently injecting further unpredictability into the present.

Finally, the move from trying to control an unpredictable future to making new ones without trying to predict any one of them requires several other rearrangements and reversals beyond those involving prediction and control. We turn next to such a rearrangement of relationships between means and ends.

2.2 Means and Ends

It is conventional to begin with a goal. In most decision-theoretic and even behavioral models, goals are given and outside the scope of the analysis. Given a goal, we can examine how to achieve it, tracing out which causes lead up to it.

Thus, goal-driven action, as depicted on the left-hand side of Figure 3, begins with a goal and then seeks means that can bring it about. Since, in many cases in

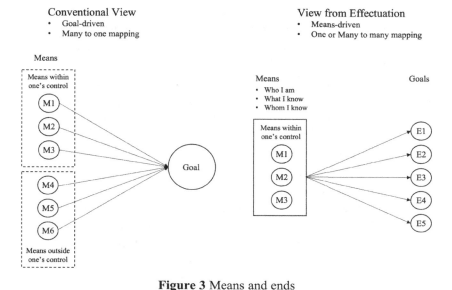

Figure 3 Means and ends

life and almost all situations in entrepreneurship, not all means necessary to the achievement of the goal will be within the control of founding entrepreneurs, they will have to engage in finding those means that are outside their control. When goal-driven, resource seeking becomes an important aspect of building new ventures. This then sets in motion the search for particular resource providers. Thus, seeking out and convincing targeted resource providers drives subgoals in new venture creation.

An effectual approach begins only with means already within the entrepreneurs' control. Entrepreneurs imagine several different possible proximate subgoals that are achievable with means already at hand. The means consist of their identity (who I am), knowledge (what I know), and network (whom I know). The ends arise from examining the question, "Given who I am, what I know and whom I know, what kinds of actions are doable and worth doing?" or "What *can* we do, given who we are, what we know and whom we know?" Notice that this can work with individual entrepreneurs as well as founding teams.

It is also possible for firms, and even communities and countries, to use this heuristic as a starting point for action. An example of this can be found in a comparative study of South Korea and Taiwan that shows how and why Taiwan specialized in higher-quality intermediate inputs, such as vehicle parts, whereas Korea built on its large, vertically integrated business groups known as "chaebol's" to produce and export higher-quality final goods, such as cars (Feenstra & Hamilton, 2006).

Additionally, the initial set of means, as described by expert entrepreneurs, does not emphasize "What I/we have." Instead, the very notion of a resource, or something owned or possessed, is seen as a function of identity, knowledge, and network. Why is this important? Because seeing resources as a creative combination of who I am, what I know, and whom I know is a way to generate a larger, more open set of possible ends. Conceptualizing resources in the more familiar sense of money or time immediately brings attention to constraints, to things that could be lost, a subject better addressed in the next section where we will examine the affordable loss principle. In contrast, identity, knowledge, and network are not depletable in the sense in which money and time may be.

This view of resources coheres much better with the way Penrose (1959) conceptualized resources than more recent views such as those found in the resource-based (Barney, 1991) or resource-dependency (Pffeffer & Salancik, 1978) views in strategic management. Resources in the Penrosean sense are versatile in a variety of different ways. For example, existing resources may be underutilized, creating slack within the system (Cyert & March, 1963/1992). Additionally, resources adapted to one use may be exaptable to other and new uses (Andreani & Cattani, 2016; Gould & Vrba, 1982). This versatility pervades effectuators' views of means-driven action. Additionally, as we will see in more depth later, this view reframes even waste and negative contingencies into positive possibilities through the affordable loss and lemonade principles respectively.

The conventional view of formulating action as goal-driven is a way of narrowing down outcome choices while broadening the need for resources. It consists of a many-to-one mapping, where all roads leading to a predetermined goal are in focus rather than the choice of the goal itself. The effectual view is means-driven and can be seen either as a many-to-many mapping, or when we consider identity, knowledge, and network as combined into a single set of means, a one-to-many mapping.

Means-driven action is narrower and more constrained in terms of resources, but it can open up and enlarge the set of possible outcomes. Since an end is not specified ex ante, unpredictability in outcomes is not seen as a problem in a means-driven approach. It is already inherent in the process. In fact, as explicated later, goal ambiguity itself becomes a resource to be leveraged through the crazy quilt principle to allow stakeholders to self-select into the effectual process. In the goal-driven case, both ends and means are constrained, even when entrepreneurs may get very creative with the way they combine their readily available means, as in the case of bricolage (Baker & Nelson, 2005; Levi-Strauss, 1966).

We need to be careful about separating means from ends in too simplistic a manner. As Simon argued, means and ends exist in hierarchies (Simon, 1964). Today's goals achieved can become tomorrow's means for achieving larger or newer goals. Similarly, today's failures can constrain tomorrow's means. Furthermore, existing knowledge of means–ends relationships constrains what is even perceived as means or as possible ends. As Gigerenzer (1991) showed through a historical analysis, tools often drive new theories, defying conventional wisdom of movement in the other direction. In any case, developments of tools and theories, means and ends, often go hand-in-hand or in iterative reflexive cycles.

Note that it is not that effectuators don't have goals or should not begin with clear goals. It is just that goals subserve means-driven action. When push comes to shove, effectuators are open to reshaping their goals rather than predicting and pursuing means not within their control. Put differently, effectuators are more tightly tethered to means than to goals, and more attentive to what is possible within their control than what may only be probable due to things outside their control.

Yet, it matters whether one approaches entrepreneurship from a goal-driven or a means-driven perspective. When entrepreneurs are closely tied to a predetermined goal, as in the case of visionary or causal approaches to venturing, their focus immediately turns to which means are necessary but not currently available. In other words, goal-driven action spotlights missing resources or the lack of needed resources, thereby reinforcing an attitude of scarcity. This awareness of scarcity further obscures ends that could be achieved with means already at hand.

2.2.1 Scarcity and Abundance

Predictive goal-driven approaches emphasize the scarcity of resources. That seems intuitive and inevitable in both practical and philosophical terms. Yet, resources can also be versatile in the sense that Penrose (1959) argued. According to this view, the notion of a resource is not static. Instead, a resource comes imbued with dynamics that allow and expand its versatility to uses that may not have originally been imagined for it (Nason & Wiklund, 2018). In this sense, there is a hidden abundance within even the scarcest of resources as they are put to new and unintended uses over time (Dew, Sarasvathy, & Venkataraman, 2004; Gould & Vrba, 1982), whether through evolutionary necessity or active human ingenuity. Moreover, the horizon of abundance is itself dynamic in the sense that it is impossible to predetermine all possible uses for resources or even for things seen as waste and therefore, by definition, not a resource at all (Karlson, Bellavitis, & France, 2021).

Human history is often the history of squeezing out abundance from within a priori scarcity, either through technological innovation or sheer street-smart creativity (Rosling, 2019; Simon, 1980). The term "productivity" in economics refers exactly to this reality (Plag, 2006). Consider the problems facing us today. Even as climate change and energy crises threaten, human imagination pushes forward toward hidden abundances in, on, and off the planet. This move toward optimism, however illusory it might in fact turn out to be, proceeds without guarantees or even positive predictions of success (Domino & Conway, 2000). At its heart, the human endeavor is effectual, even when it draws from and builds on the other three quadrants in the prediction-control space.

One concrete way this attitude of abundance bears fruit in the effectual process is by reducing the time to action. When tied to means already within one's control, there is no excuse for postponing action. Entrepreneurs don't have to wait to get missing resources in place before building ventures. By untethering themselves from preset goals, they become free to achieve the immediately achievable. Furthermore, by simply ignoring resources not currently on hand, they begin to strengthen their attention to possibility rather than impossibility or improbability. Such a bias for action also moves them into situations requiring improvisation, exaptation, and resourcefulness of other kinds. Situations of scarcity become interesting challenges to be overcome rather than paralyzing excuses for inaction or waiting for the perfect moment to act.

This raises the specter of overoptimism (Van den Steen, 2004) and other biases that entrepreneurs have been shown to be subject to (Camerer & Lovallo, 1999; Koellinger, Minniti, & Schade, 2007). Although most human beings, including entrepreneurs, may be subject to biases of one kind or another, scholars have also argued that bias research itself may be biased in a variety of ways so as to obscure the ecological rationality that offers useful alternatives (Gigerenzer, 2018). Additionally, given the effectual problem space consisting of Knightian uncertainty, goal ambiguity, and isotropy, it is not clear what would count as bias-free behavior (Hayward et al., 2010).

2.2.2 Can and Should

Being means-driven also implies a move away from the normative to the possible. Being goal-driven not only spotlights what is missing from our extant set of resources but also shuts out or hides from our view paths not leading to the goal that may nonetheless be worth pursuing if only one could see and reflect upon them. In other words, in goal-driven approaches, our assessments hinge on what should and should not be done in light of the goal being pursued. The clear and shining goal beckons us normatively, obscuring and making alternative paths more costly. In light of this, better prediction comes to be seen not only as useful but necessary in minimizing those costs. Novice entrepreneurs often worry about the best possible course of action, striving to avoid distraction along the shortest path to the goal. This blinds them to the fact that some of those distractions may, in fact, hold uncalculated benefits.

One discussion that often comes up with people contemplating becoming an entrepreneur concerns the opportunity cost of starting a venture (Amit, Muller, & Cockburn, 1995; Cassar, 2006). Anyone with a well-paying job confronts this problem. This problem is studied in economics under the rubric of occupational choice (Wong, Lee, & Der Foo, 2008). The argument from opportunity cost goes as follows: If I am to leave my job to start a venture, I have to ensure that the venture will make at least as much money as my current job. Given that entrepreneurs do not always make more money than they might have in a wage job, this literature explains their decision to start a venture in terms of a love of risk-taking, overconfidence, or an irrational failure to take opportunity costs into account. A more positive explanation consists in the possibility that the gap between the opportunity cost and the return on venturing is filled by psychological payoffs of some kind, being one's own boss, for example.

One way to bring the effectual view of this into focus is by simply evoking the inverse question, "What is your opportunity cost of NOT starting a venture, or not becoming an entrepreneur?" There are two aspects of the problem that are highlighted through the discussion of this question. First, it is easier to compute the opportunity cost of starting a venture simply because of the assumption that the wage market is somehow predictable and will remain so indefinitely. It is important to explicate this assumption since there is a nonzero probability that it is not justified. Second, there is an asymmetry in the probability distribution on the venturing decision. While there is no certainty that an entrepreneur will make any money at all, it is certain she will not gain the rewards of entrepreneurship if she does not venture. On one side is an uncertain gain, and, on the other, a certain loss. Framed this way, the two-sided opportunity cost question becomes nonobvious, even tantalizing.

Therefore, it is not useful to frame the problem in terms of whether one should or should not start a venture. It is more worthwhile instead to consider how one can or cannot get it going, rather than whether one should or shouldn't.

Normatively speaking, a goal-driven approach assumes that not being tethered to clear goals can lead one astray. Seen from this perspective, the effectual approach seems to be tinged with a flavor of irreverence, if not complete recklessness. Is proceeding without clear goals merely a matter of aimless wandering? Brownian motion? A form of hopeless optimism?

We have to acknowledge the possibility that an unmooring from goals can be problematic in many ways, including walking into dead ends. However, it is also important to note that the effectual approach is not one of merely not having a goal. Instead, it is a tool to generate goals worth pursuing, with or without broader purposes clarified at the beginning of action. Effectual action is tied to means within one's control. It is means-*driven*. This suggests a conscious choice to take viable action (doing what can be done) with normative concerns (what ought to be done) becoming guideposts in the fashioning of new goals, fabricated and refined through means-driven action, which brings us to conceptualizations of preferences and values.

2.2.3 Preferences and Values

There exist large literatures on preferences and values (Edwards & Fasolo, 2001; Hastie, 2001). Whereas values are often discussed in terms of virtue, consequentialist, and deontological philosophies in business ethics (Chakrabarty & Bass, 2015), preferences are either deemed arbitrary or arising from evolutionary and cultural path dependencies (Hechter & Kanazawa, 1997; Stigler & Becker, 1977). Here I use a practical way to think about the two without assuming specific sources for either, yet allowing the two to interact within the prediction-control space.

Preferences refer to things we want, while values concern things we believe we ought to want. We may prefer junk food while knowing that we should be eating spinach instead for its nutritional value. Preferences and values thus offer a different instantiation of can versus should. The notion of value here can take the place of a valuable goal, with preferences competing with it, setting up trade-offs and lobbing hurdles along paths to its achievement. But this way of approaching preferences and values sets up a false dichotomy, leading to absurdities such as economic versus social values or maximizing profits versus maximizing welfare and well-being. In the following, even when I use these conventionally understood meanings of the terms preferences and values, I do not want us to lose sight of the fact that both these and other related terms are forged through the dynamic interactions within the prediction-control space and the coevolution of the space itself in grappling with its encompassing uncertainties.

In the effectual means set, the "who I am" can contain both preferences and values, conventionally understood. So, how do we reconcile the effectual starting point if these are in opposition? Expert entrepreneurs tend to be clearer about their values, viewing preferences as more malleable. Not necessarily because they are better people, but simply because of concrete experiences navigating the prediction-control space. As a result, they also tend to define values more clearly in terms of what they will not do or what is nonnegotiable for them – a set of constraints on action rather than in positive terms that shape specific goals.

A useful example of this could be constraints on eating junk food without specifying the imperative to eat spinach. This formulation removes the straw-man dichotomy of chips versus spinach while opening our palate to explore healthier alternatives. It transforms a choice between two bads or even between a good and a bad into a more open choice between other goods that bridge preferences and values. Such a creative focus on doability and openness allows people to specify the constraint in terms of can (I can sometimes replace soda with juice and add a salad to my meal) rather than should (I need to eat spinach, which I abhor, or never drink soda).

Intellectually, we tend to give in to the temptation to model preferences and values as clear from the beginning and consistent over time. In reality, both are forged and reshaped through movements within the prediction-control space. This can be messy to begin with and grow messier in efforts to clarify and cocreate over time. Yet, the very inconsistencies we seek to avoid in our modeling efforts can fertilize the space toward new values worth striving for.

Thus, effectuation combines a focus on viable, means-driven action with an explicit acknowledgment of futures that are constructible through action and interaction. This means that both preferences and values can be cocreated over time. More specifically, values can be shaped into new goals, even when their viability is constrained through initial preferences opposed to them. This seeming tug-of-war between viability and value is tilted even more toward value as we proceed with considerations of affordable loss and the nuances of effectual interactions with others, who self-select into the shaping of ends worth achieving. We turn to the former in the next section.

2.3 Risk and Return

Figure 4 depicts the standard conceptualization of the risk curve with Return on the vertical axis and Risk (usually measured as volatility in finance or, more generally, variance in statistics) on the horizontal axis.

In this view, most theories begin with the predicted linear relationship along the 45-degree angle, wherein higher risks are associated with higher returns and lower returns are associated with lower risks (Chang & Pinegar, 1988; Markowitz, 1991). The intuition here is that returns compensate for risks taken. This not only has the advantage of serving to incentivize necessary risk-taking, without which we cannot survive as a species or an economy, but also has the virtue of earners of higher returns "deserving" the returns they earn, as justified compensation for risks they dared to take.

In terms of incentives, this intuition is embodied in the "efficient frontier" (Gollinger & Morgan, 1993) typically shown in the risk–return space as the curve along the northwest in the top-left quadrant of Figure 4. Both investment managers and managers of companies they invest in seek to get onto that efficient frontier. Portfolios that fall below that curve are considered suboptimal. Unintended behavioral consequences ensue, as they almost always do in the face of optimal goals. Investors often interpret risk-taking as a necessary, even desirable course of action. Venture capitalists get comfortable with nine out of ten investments failing, even though the failure rate of non-venture capital funded ventures is almost the inverse of this number (Nielsen & Sarasvathy, 2018). We will look into this in a bit more detail in Section 2.5.

In a think-aloud experimental study comparing bankers with entrepreneurs, my coauthors Lester Lave and Herbert Simon and I found a set of interesting differences in how these two groups perceived and managed both financial and nonfinancial risks (Sarasvathy, Simon, & Lave, 1998). I have summarized the results from that study as the two straight, perpendicular arrows in Figure 4. We found that bankers began with a desired level of expected return and then suggested ways to reduce risk (horizontal arrow going from right to left) through strategies such as diversification and staging of investments into smaller chunks, something akin to real options. In contrast, entrepreneurs accepted a minimal level of risk beyond which they did not want to go and then came up with creative ideas to increase return (vertical arrow going from bottom to top).

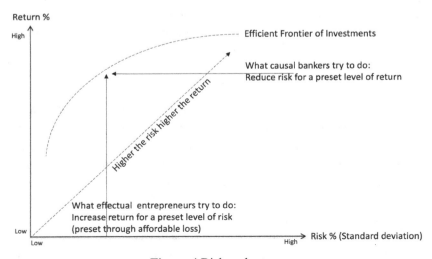

Figure 4 Risk and return

It is easy to see why bankers would feel no control over increasing returns but nonetheless believe they could control risk. Since this study preceded my dissertation that led to the discovery of effectual reasoning, it was not easy to see why entrepreneurs would feel they could change/increase the expected return on low-risk projects. It was also not easy to see why they would choose low-risk projects in the first place.

With the toolbox of effectuation, both of these results are explained: the former in terms of the pilot-in-the-plane principle, and the latter in terms of affordable loss. In other words, entrepreneurs have a worldview in which new futures are cocreated rather than predicted. That opens up ways to control and shape returns. At the same time, this also sensitizes them to the inefficacy of predictions and hence the inadvisability of placing large bets or being risk-takers in the conventional sense of the term. This explains their preference for lower risk.

At the time we completed the study of bankers and entrepreneurs, dominant theories in entrepreneurship and finance were arguing that entrepreneurs were risk-takers (Brockhaus, 1980; MacCrimmon & Wehrung, 1990). On average, entrepreneurs were hypothesized to score higher on measures of risk propensity when compared with the general, non-entrepreneurial population. Bankers, according to conventional wisdom, were likely risk-averse, even more than non-bankers. Our findings contradicted conventional wisdom on both sides.

Once we move these findings into the prediction-control space, however, these findings are no longer surprising. Bankers have developed a belief in predictive control and some degree of competence in risk prevention strategies. Entrepreneurs have learned non-predictive (effectual) control, refusing to trust expected return calculations but building competence in shaping higher returns without taking much risk. That is why entrepreneurs tackling the structured tasks in the study began by choosing projects with the lowest level of risk.

Interestingly, in our study of bankers and entrepreneurs, these attitudes and approaches to risk and return carried through to nonfinancial risks as well. Without belaboring the point, effectual entrepreneurs challenge the traditional relationship illustrated through the 45-degree line in Figure 4. While venture capitalists may only make supranormal returns by taking large risks across multiple ventures, most of which tend to fail, entrepreneurs cannot invest in multiple ventures. Instead, they reduce the risks they take to their affordable loss and "make" higher returns through the effectual process.

The entrepreneurs' only alternative to effectual cocreation of returns is to hope that their single bet (or very few bets) would somehow hit the jackpot. Expert entrepreneurs reject the latter. As one of them put it, "If you want to place a bet, go to Vegas. Starting a company is nothing like rolling the dice."

This rearrangement of the risk–return relationship has wide-ranging implications not only in entrepreneurship and finance but also in the lives of individuals and societies. At first glance, it may seem too good to be true to think that we can systematically combine low risk with high return. To see how this can be accomplished, we need to unpack both concepts. Let us begin with risk.

The notion of risk as deviations from expectations in predicted distributions of returns is a very narrow conceptualization. In the lives of individuals and societies, risks are often multifaceted and interact in multiple ways (Bromiley & Curley, 1992; March & Shapira, 1987; Yates, 1992). For example, the same person who is risk-averse when it comes to finance may be a risk-taker in sporting activities or other behaviors such as smoking or dating. Risk-taking also changes with life stage and in response to life events.

Risk-taking varies over the lifetime of the same individual. Single young people may take risks that their parents may not in later life. Yet parents may take risks that young people ignore. In fact, just the decision to have a child entails important risks, such as hazards to the mother's health and a nonzero probability of children with severe physical and mental disabilities. At the other end of the spectrum, empty nesters may grow more risk-averse over time. Alternatively, they could throw caution to the winds as they age and take on risky projects in retirement. So too with societies. Democracies are often born in revolutions, requiring a high level of risk-taking to overthrow tyranny. But more mature societies may become risk-averse, resulting in complacency and even apathy, leading to declines in democracy itself.

Criticisms of gross oversimplification notwithstanding, the point here is that the conceptualization of risk as volatility in expected return may be too thin a concept for picturing real-world spaces for managing risk and return. This point is important in conceptualizations of return as well. Returns too are multifaceted and multidimensional, changing over life and circumstance. In fact, a careful examination of the most impactful advances in knowledge or human well-being shows that not only is it difficult to specify returns or beneficial consequences in advance, it may also be impossible to even imagine, let alone predict them ex ante (Crisp, 2021; Langer, 2005).

History is strewn with examples of unpredictability, both in risks and returns (Beatty & Carrera, 2011). This unpredictability often takes the form of Knightian uncertainty, thwarting the very attempt to conceptualize a risk–return space in the first place.

Yet, what we need here is not to simply throw away risk–return calculations. These calculations are still useful in predictable situations. What we need is to deepen our understanding of a more pluralistic conceptualization of multiple layers of risks and returns, and how they interact with control and changing goals. Additionally, there are ecological and behavioral aspects at work in the risk–return space.

2.3.1 Gains and Losses

One of the most influential ideas in behavioral economics is prospect theory (Kahneman & Tversky, 1979). This empirically well-supported theory shows that human beings value losses and gains differently. For example, people experience a loss of five dollars as much more painful than any pleasure they feel from a gain of five dollars. In other words, human behavior exhibits a disproportionately higher aversion to loss than joy in an equivalent gain.

This raises an important question for the affordable loss principle in effectuation. While it is rather intuitive to see that some proportion of individuals in any given population may be risk-loving, it is harder to see how a risk-averse person may choose and implement the affordable loss principle of effectuation. The former simply builds on the inherent variation in the human population. In that view, entrepreneurs are drawn from the risk-taker segment. Furthermore, they could suffer from overconfidence or overoptimism bias and so chase after high returns even in the face of high risks. But the argument that entrepreneurs choose to lose something, not just take risks, has to answer the challenge from prospect theory that human behavior is loss-averse.

The obvious answer is in the concept "affordable" loss. Once we give up preset relationships between risk and return, we have made the same kind of move with risk and return that we did with prediction and control. Risks and returns, in effectuation, can be broken up into separate categories and treated in disparate ways. Entrepreneurs then seek to avoid losses they wish to avoid by not including them in their calculations of affordable loss.

In fact, expert entrepreneurs suggest that starting with as close to zero investment as possible, for example, with nothing more than a small amount of time, is a level of loss everyone can afford. This has the added advantage of forcing effectual entrepreneurs to become creative and cocreative. When they do choose to invest something more than zero, the affordable loss heuristic not only allows them to keep the downside within their control but also impels them to consider why a venture might be worth doing even when it does not succeed (Dew et al., 2009).

Here it is useful to bring to mind the difference between heuristic and algorithm. Unlike algorithms that are sought in the external data in the world, heuristics are shorthand rules-of-thumb *constructed* by actors learning from their experiences. In other words, heuristics are mental artifacts and not naturally existing patterns "out there" in the world waiting to be discovered. That is why, as

Spender (2013: 323) explains, " ... even without being able to specify the processes involved in searching, perceiving, memorizing, and learning, one could probe these mental artefacts as an actors' rules-in-use in domains other than chess and logic proofs—especially in economic and organizational activity."

Keeping in mind this understanding of heuristics, we can notice that affordable loss framing need not contradict with theories of loss aversion (Martina, 2018). Instead, it is a way of learning to put loss aversion to work in tackling uncertainty. Let's reconsider the decision to leave a job to start a venture. Prospect theory suggests that most people would be more averse to the possible loss of their wage income than the possible yet uncertain gain from their venture. The affordable loss heuristic reframes the problem as follows: If I start a venture, I may or may not gain a large income. But if I do not start one, I will certainly lose the possibility to profit from my venture, but more importantly, never become an entrepreneur. This framing uncovers the fact that there are losses on both sides of the equation. In other words, within the affordable loss heuristic, loss aversion can cut both ways.

In fact, as mentioned earlier, the conscious choice of paying attention to loss and moving forward in spite of it can free up the creative and cocreative potential within human beings. Thinking through what one is willing and able to lose for the venture enables effectual entrepreneurs to notice slack in the system and in their own lives. It cues in a sensibility for imagining resources and opportunities where they might otherwise have only seen scarcity and constraints.

Pitches to potential stakeholders can also imbue this sensibility. In the traditional conceptualization of risk and return, entrepreneurs tend to pitch the upside: the expected return wrapped up in strategies to mitigate predicted risks. The aim is to make a compelling case for why any targeted stakeholder should invest their resources in the (risky) new venture.

In the effectual approach, entrepreneurs can make the additional "why not" pitch. They can ask people to invest no more than they can afford to lose. This can include slack resources, which are currently not being put to use, or simply investing nonfinancial resources or engaging in some form of barter in return for sweat equity from the entrepreneur. The iconic example here is that of Richard Branson asking Boeing to let him lease a couple of airplanes to start Virgin Atlantic. The deal was to return the planes if the venture did not work out. We will explore this in terms of pitch versus ask in Section 2.4.1.

2.4 Competition and Commitment/Collusion

The concept of competition is central to understandings of free markets, whether in the neoclassical sense of perfect competition or more nuanced versions that include innovation and imperfect information. The canonical illustration of competition in strategic management is encapsulated in Porter's five forces framework, depicted on the right-hand side of Figure 5 (Porter, 2008). In this framework, an industry or market is characterized not only by competitive rivalry from within but is also subject to external threats from all four sides: new entrants and substitutes, as well as the differential bargaining power of suppliers and customers. Note that this framework does not and cannot explain how markets come to be in the first place.

The effectual framework precedes Porter by offering a view of how new markets are cocreated in the first place by entrepreneurs and their stakeholders. There are two important points to note here. First, entrepreneurial ventures are not merely captured in the term "new entrants" as in the Porter framework. Second, the particular role of a stakeholder, whether a supplier or a customer or something else, is not given or assumed a priori in the effectual framework. Instead, the effectual process transforms a variety of readily available means into a new market through people self-selecting into stakeholder roles in the process through specific commitments. These commitments not only determine the resources coming into the new market but also explain and cocreate all five forces of the Porter framework. In this sense, the effectual process offers a framework of self-selective collusion rather than competition.

Effectuation could thus be seen as a framework of self-organization. It offers a view of how all kinds of people living their various lives can, at times, coalesce into new ventures and markets. This can happen intentionally, with entrepreneurs kick-starting the process with their bird-in-hand. But it can also occur contingently, with the process beginning anywhere in the effectual process diagram. Entrepreneurship history is rife with stories of chance encounters between people leading to ideas and actions for new ventures (Dew, 2009; Koehn, 2001; Shah & Tripsas, 2007). Take the case of Microsoft, for instance. Although Gates and Allen were writing code in their own venture, the deal with IBM that helped them "make the big time" happened because their competitor, Gary Kildall, had blown off his meeting with IBM (Allen, 2012).

Whether intentionally forged or contingently cocreated, each effectual commitment resolves a variety of components, such as resources, relationships, roles, and responsibilities, that feed into new markets emerging from interactions between self-selecting stakeholders. Entrepreneurs, in this view, consist of one kind of stakeholder. The specific commitments in the effectual process result in the formulation of new entrants and substitutes, as depicted in the Porter framework. The commitments also specify roles for incoming stakeholders and relational structures between stakeholders, such as suppliers and customers. Finally, commitments determine who colludes with whom and who

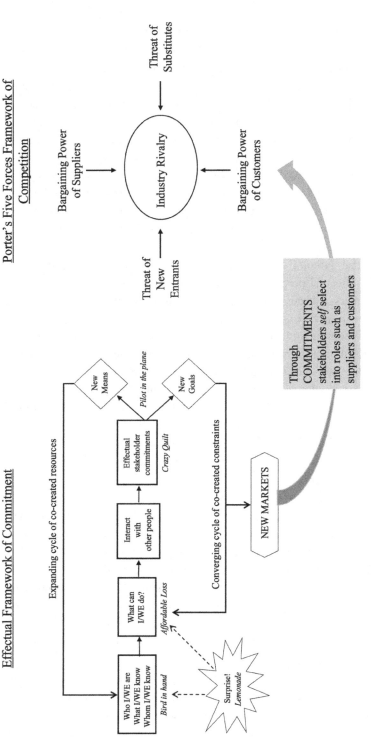

Figure 5 Competition and commitment

does not. It is, therefore, possible to undertake an effectual analysis of how and why specific industries emerge into competitive spaces of the kind we see within the five forces framework.

Traditionally, a slew of benefits have been attributed to competitive forces. Classical economists debated and discussed the benefits of the "invisible hand," namely doing away with the need for a central authority to manage the economy (Smith, 1863). Under the school of neoclassical economics, these benefits were formalized through equilibrium (Arrow & Debreu, 1954; Marshall, 1890 [2009]) and optimality conditions, showing that given certain reasonable assumptions, free competition could ensure at least that no one got worse off (Pareto, Schwier, & Page, 1971). In the twentieth century, Hayek (1984) and Schumpeter (1975[1942]) moved beyond neoclassical conceptualizations of perfectly competitive markets, to argue for the innovative potential of competitive markets, even when not entirely perfect.

How does a collusive or even a cocreative framework play into and alter these benefits? First, it should be noted that competition is a characteristic of markets and may be theorized in terms of the behavior of participants in existing markets, such as suppliers and buyers. This does not necessarily mean that competitive behavior is ubiquitous or even necessary in the *origin* of new markets. Nor does this suggest or assume any reasons for why people should behave competitively. Most importantly, competitive and cooperative behaviors interact in interesting ways even within existing markets (Brandenburger & Nalebuff, 1996).

Adam Smith himself argued for a more nuanced understanding of human behavior and interaction as the basis for exchanges in market economies:

> "... *different genius is not the foundation of this disposition to barter which is the cause of the division of labour. The real foundation of it is that principle to perswade which so much prevails in human nature ... We ought then to mainly cultivate the power to perswasion* ..." (Adam Smith, 1766, "Lectures in jurisprudence," p. 551)

Current and potential competitors can become self-selecting stakeholders in the effectual process, colluding to cocreate new markets. As we showed in great detail and depth in Sarasvathy and Dew (2005), effectual commitments are crucial in the face of Knightian uncertainty. And by definition, it is not possible to compete in a market that does not yet exist and whose shape and boundaries cannot be specified ex ante. However, as the new market begins to take shape and coagulate into more predictable boundaries, competitive entry increases to manifest the rivalry that we see in most extant markets and in the Porter framework.

A telling example of the reality of cocreation masked by a theory of competition can be found in Brian Loasby's historical examination of Schumpeter's example of creative destruction (Loasby, 1999; 2001). In his famous chapter on this idea, Schumpeter used the example of railroads replacing horse carriages as evidence for his argument supporting the creative–destructive force of innovation. When Loasby studied the actual history of these two industries, he found that the manufacturers of horse carriages simply retooled their facilities to make railroad carriages. While it appeared that technological innovation had destroyed firms in the horse carriage industry, in reality, several of the very same firms from the old industry cocreated the new one, learning from each other to transform resources already within their control.

Why are commitments crucial to action in the face of Knightian uncertainty? The answer is that by simply agreeing to act in predictable ways, we can impose predictability. In other words, effectual commitments can sometimes transform uncertainties into reliable predictions. A simple example from daily life may suffice. For those of us who grew up and learned to drive in places like Mumbai, the daily commute can be a matter of unpredictability, even bordering on Knightian uncertainty. Yet, as I was astonished to learn during my first visit outside India to Germany, it is possible to create predictability through traffic lights, but only to the extent that people commit to heeding them.

The larger lesson here is that in several domains of human action, actual commitments between stakeholders can cocreate valuable structures that obviate the necessity to predict the future, at costs that can be affordable.

In the case of effectual entrepreneurship, this can be even more beneficial since the process is more like shaping something out of clay than traversing environments largely given and outside the control of individual commuters. Spatial metaphors, such as fields of discovery, can benefit both from commitment frameworks as well as frameworks of competition. But in the face of Knightian uncertainty, transformative metaphors involving shaping and making something new are more useful than motifs of discovery.

In fact, as I have argued elsewhere and will again in Section 2.6, markets are not naturally occurring arenas within which competition happens. Markets are artifacts shaped and formed through human action and interaction. The benefits of competition depend in important ways on humans' ability to collude and cocreate through non-predictive (effectual) commitments. Let's turn to an examination of how exactly these commitments come to be.

2.4.1 Pitch and Ask

Commitments can be part of an exchange, but they can also be simply a matter of making things – things such as products and services, governance structures, and organizational forms, even interim prototypes for any of these. To understand them, we cannot begin with the familiar economic primitive of an exchange. We need to start with a pre-exchange primitive, such as the one of "persuasion" alluded to earlier by Adam Smith.

The notion of a "pitch" immediately comes to mind. A pitch is a form of communication between an entrepreneur and a targeted stakeholder (Huang & Knight, 2017). Pitches usually contain a description of something the pitcher wants from the target and can include reasons why the targeted stakeholders should assent to the pitch. Reasons can include items of exchange, such as a concurrent quid pro quo or a share in future rewards. However, the pitch assumes that the pitcher knows what she wants and also has reasonably accurate estimates of what the targeted stakeholder might want. Moreover, the pitcher also has to have prior knowledge of whom to target in the first place.

In contrast, the effectual entrepreneur talks to anyone and everyone. How can she even craft a pitch? In practice, the answer is that she doesn't. Effectual entrepreneurs simply ask, rather than pitch. Asking generalizes the pitch to the non-predictive quadrants of the prediction-control space. Asks can range from asking for advice, feedback, information, and help to asking to cocreate something/anything together. In other words, the pitch is a special kind of ask. When the asker knows exactly what to ask for, from whom, and how, she can make a pitch.

The ask is a very generalized pre-exchange phenomenon that routinely occurs in the lives of all people, in and out of the entrepreneurial context. A subset of them might eventually turn into pitches. Another important subset consists of effectual asks that fabricate commitments that feed into the cocreation of new markets and ventures.

Note that both pitches and asks involve resources and relationships, but the directionality between resources and relationships is reversed in the effectual case. While the pitch postulates resources as the objective, with relationships hitching a ride on those resources, the effectual ask views relationships as the objective, with resources opening the door to them and coming along for the ride. As one expert entrepreneur put it, "People chase wallets. They don't realize wallets come with faces. And sometimes you learn the hard way that it's miserable to face those faces. So why not chase faces? Faces come with wallets too, even if those might be smaller."

This raises an interesting question: Why would anyone want to commit to an entrepreneur or a new venture without clear predictions of risk-adjusted rewards? To unpack this, we need to examine the role of self-interest and altruism in human interactions.

2.4.2 Opportunism and Altruism

Maybe the notion of self-interest being the default basis for human behavior began with the overused quote from Adam Smith about the butcher, the brewer, and the baker in Chapter 2 of the *Wealth of Nations* (Smith, 1863). But historically speaking, Smith wrote *Moral Sentiments* before *Wealth of Nations* (Smith, 1822). A richer, more textured view of human behavior is evident there, as well as in many other writings of Adam Smith, as we saw in the quote about "persuasion" used earlier.

Herbert Simon returned to an examination of Smith's works in 1997 (Simon, 1997, p. 5–9). What prompted his, and in turn my, attention to Smith's observations about human behavior was the ubiquitous assumption of self-interested behavior in *Homo Economicus*, and the normative idea from Williamson that contracts should be written with an eye to opportunism (Williamson, 1993). Opportunism, defined as self-interest seeking with guile (Williamson, 1985), pervades theories in strategic management and has also influenced entrepreneurship. This takes the form of quid pro quo incorporated into pitches, as well as paranoid obsessions with the prospect of potential stakeholders stealing one's venture idea or other intellectual property. Williamson's urging of writing contracts with a view to opportunistic behavior has also influenced legal issues surrounding new venture creation and funding.

Yet, I found that expert entrepreneurs were deeply skeptical of investments in intellectual property protection, nondisclosure agreements, and other ways to preempt opportunism. They seemed perversely open to interacting with anyone and everyone, seeking to build corridors along which potential stakeholders can walk through doors they deliberately left open. Yet, this is not an attitude of naïve or ideological altruism. Instead, it is an implementation of Simon's concept of intelligent altruism.

Intelligent altruism is the idea that human beings have evolved to develop an intuitive sense of when to be altruistic and when not to be (Simon, 1997). This intuition is further reinforced and refined through social experiences. The depth and breadth of experiences expert entrepreneurs have encountered in building and running new ventures, beginning with the simple ask and pitch to nuanced effectual asks, have fine-tuned their intelligent altruism to ways of talking, acting, and interacting that lead to actual commitments. The commitments themselves offer parameters for structuring initial deals and forging longer-term relationships without having to plan against predicted opportunistic behavior.

Instead of continually worrying about opportunism, expert entrepreneurs recognize the behavioral mechanism that drives intelligent altruism. Simon dubbed this "docility" – a term inspired by Adam Smith's observations and referring to the fact that human beings are both persuadable and persuasive (Knudsen, 2003). It is easy to see how this concept can be embodied in the effectual ask. Without imposing any necessary conditions on whom to interact with or what their preferences might be, the effectual ask cues in altruism and walls off opportunism through the simple embrace of not predicting or promising specific upsides. Instead, only those who believe for reasons of their own that a particular commitment at any given point of time in a venturing relationship is worthwhile will self-select into the effectual process. Affordable loss further facilitates such commitments by compelling stakeholders to confront the possibility of losing whatever they commit.

It is important to note that as the venture begins to coalesce into specific products and stakeholder networks that shape its environment into a more predictable space, opportunists will be able to erode the wall that kept them out initially. As the process on the left-hand side of Figure 5 evolves into the five forces on the right-hand side, techniques to avoid and overcome opportunistic behavior might become more salient. However, expert entrepreneurs offer ways to develop an organizational culture that embodies and encourages intelligent altruism. Iconic examples of these include AES Corporation, Medtronic, and more recently Basecamp.

2.4.3 Persistence and Quitting

One interesting question that often arises in the context of the crazy quilt principle is how the effectual process might end or whether it suffers from a "halting" problem,[2] leading to unproductive churn (Fischer & Reuber, 2011; Kerr & Coviello, 2019). This question has to do with a perception that the effectual process continuously offers up new goals and new stakeholders, none of which may actually lead to an enduring profitable venture. This question arises because of confounding the effectual approach with the visionary and/or the adaptive.

The visionary entrepreneur persists against all odds. In confounding that with effectuation, it is easy to fall into the idea that entrepreneurs have to accept any and all stakeholders who wish to self-select into the process. In contrast, the adaptive entrepreneur continually gathers information and advice and pivots to new ideas based on these inputs. Again, confounding the adaptive approach with the effectual suggests that endless new ideas and new goals can arise without any of these getting implemented into a productive enterprise.

---

[2] According to Wikipedia, "In computability theory, the halting problem is the problem of determining, from a description of an arbitrary computer program and an input, whether the program will finish running, or continue to run forever. Alan Turing proved in 1936 that a general algorithm to solve the halting problem for all possible program-input pairs cannot exist."

These two forms of confusion sometimes come from academic theories of entrepreneurship, such as personality traits in psychology relating to persistence, passion, grit, and so on (Cardon & Kirk, 2015; Holland & Shepherd, 2013; Mooradian et al., 2016), or from popular practitioner prescriptions, such as the notion of pivoting (Grimes, 2018). Additionally, these misconceptions can also occur in the way entrepreneurs recount their experiences. Experienced entrepreneurs will often urge others to be persistent, to persevere in their ventures without regard to cost. One early academic definition of entrepreneurship echoes this bromide: *The process by which individuals – either on their own or inside organizations – pursue opportunities without regard to the resources they currently control* (Stevenson & Jarillo, 1990, p. 23).

I once heard an entrepreneur use the analogy of the pit bull that never gives up. Paradoxically, the very same entrepreneur remarked a little later in his talk that one has to know when to quit. Since then, I started to take note of such paradoxical statements in the data we have collected over the past two decades. Effectual entrepreneurship offers at least two ways for this particular paradox to be resolved.

First, by committing no more than they can afford to lose. For example, if an effectuator decides ahead of time to spend six months of nights and weekends and no more than $5,000 to try and build a venture, during those six months and until that $5,000 runs out, she can persist without second-guessing her decision to start the venture. However, if and when she runs out of her affordable loss limits, she seriously considers quitting. This can halt the effectual process.

Second, when entrepreneurs pursue their ventures effectually, their affordable loss levels would likely increase through commitments from self-selected stakeholders, each of whom may invest no more than *they* can afford to lose. This allows the venture to persist beyond the initial affordable loss limits. However, every stakeholder in the process, including the founding entrepreneurs, can always choose not to accept a commitment from an incoming stakeholder, thereby halting the effectual process.

Once we unpack different approaches to building new ventures within the prediction-control space, it becomes easier to see that neither persistence nor pivoting is an issue in effectual entrepreneurship. In fact, constraints intrinsic to the principles can work as useful valves to turn persistence on and off. Pivots are a nonissue since the effectual process can only move forward through actual commitments that underwrite the next step/s and not through mere information, advice, or feedback. Unless a large variety of stakeholders make several different commitments, endlessly pivoting is not a part of the effectual process. Furthermore, every time a commitment occurs, both parties involved (incoming stakeholders and extant entrepreneurs) now have to deliver on the commitment, thereby limiting their ability to engage in new commitments. In summary, effectual commitments make the process convergent to cocreation, rather than divergent to multiple pivots, each of which rests on shifting sands of prediction.

However, whether and when to refuse a commitment from a self-selected stakeholder remains an unexamined question in effectuation research. Here, the bird-in-hand principle is likely the most relevant lever. When incoming stakeholders do not align with the "who we are" aspect of the bird-in-hand, current stakeholders, including the entrepreneur, may walk away. This can occur through conflicts in values and preferences or relational mismatches. On the flip side, expert entrepreneurs will go to great lengths to deliver on commitments they have agreed to, thereby strengthening persistence and perseverance. Sometimes, this can be a hard lesson for novices, leading them to escalation of commitment beyond their affordable loss.

The key point to note here is that the effectual approach does not extol persistence or other related traits for its own sake. In fact, the very idea of affordable loss is to ensure that quitting is always an option in effectuation.

We have so far considered voluntary exit. How about involuntary exit?

2.5 Success and Failure

In practice, entrepreneurs will sometimes assert that "failure is not an option." This is often countered in academia with the snarky, seemingly empirical rejoinder, "most firms fail." It turns out that both of these statements are misleading in an eerily similar way. The first is misleading because what expert entrepreneurs mean when they say "failure is not an option" is that success–failure is not a 0-1 variable. The second is misleading when it confounds the success/failure of the entrepreneur with the success/failure of the firm.

As I argued in the previous section, expert entrepreneurs learn that failure is always an option, even when they may claim in public pronouncements to the contrary. One example of reality, as opposed to retrospective claims, comes from the history of eBay:

> So far, the skeptics had been right. Along with his informal attempts at word-of-mouth promotion, Omidyar had been announcing the launch of Internet directories that listed new websites. "The most fun buying and selling on the web!" he gushed in one post, though AuctionWeb had thus far been the site of few sales and not much fun. Back then, everyone with a domain name and a server to host it was trying to get a website off the ground. It looked like AuctionWeb would be just another one of the hordes that faded away for lack of interest.
> The truth was, that was just fine with Omidyar. When he had banged out the computer code for AuctionWeb over Labor Day weekend, he thought of it as a hobby and a chance to practice programming for the Internet. He certainly

never considered quitting his day job. Just keeping the site running and pulling it back up from its constant crashes was taking up most of his time, and Omidyar was not the workaholic type. Failure was definitely an option. (Cohen, 2003)

Figure 6 contrasts the view from effectuation on the right-hand side with the standard one of success–failure as a 0-1 option. The standard depiction on the left-hand side incorporates the probability of success and the probability of failure, adding up to 1. This means that failure may be defined as not succeeding, and success can be considered not failing. While this conceptualization may be useful for certain kinds of formal modeling of performance, there is something clearly missing from it from an experiential point of view. Not merely entrepreneurial experience, but human experience more generally, suggests a more nuanced view (Petroski, 1985; Roberts, 1989). Hence, our engagement with psychological variables such as persistence, grit, resilience, and so on.

Ordinary life is filled with failures, opening doors to eventual success. Instances also abound of success leading to negative consequences, ranging from simple bad behavior to debilitating relational failures. It could be argued that we need to keep definitions simple and measurable. Therefore, confounding relational and other types of psychosocial aspects of performance with simple firm performance obscures the point. While simple firm performance statistics may be the starting point (even that is not that "simple" as we will see later), several other variables are crucial for theorizing as well as teaching. Moreover, entrepreneurs cannot afford to concern themselves only with firm performance.

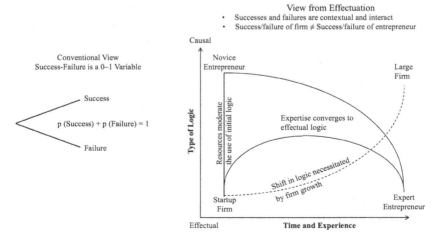

Figure 6 Success and failure

How they think and feel about it, and relate to others through those cognitions and emotions, has a real impact on whether they succeed or fail. Hence, a deeper dive is warranted.

In order to develop an understanding of the two effectual models on the right-hand side of Figure 6, one relating to firm performance and the other to the careers of entrepreneurs, we will take a much deeper dive into the very notion of success and failure. Over the past decade, several studies in entrepreneurship have begun mapping out the landscape of entrepreneurial performance (Audretsch, Santarelli, & Vivarelli, 1999; OECD, 2015, 2016). Consider the statement alluded to earlier, "most firms fail." In one sense, this statement is correct; most firms do not exist forever. Even in the short term, about half the firms that get started will disappear. However, that does not always mean failure. The term "exit" is more appropriate. Consider, for example, that of the 50 percent or so of firms that exit, a third are profitable at the time of exit (Headd, 2003).

Firms exit for a variety of voluntary and semi-voluntary reasons, some professional and others personal. On the personal front, these can range from the life stage of founders to job opportunities that pay more than the venture under certain macroeconomic conditions (Luzzi & Sasson, 2016) to life events such as death, marriage, divorce, and parenting (Wennberg et al., 2010). Conflicts and clashes between founding team members form one of the most prevalent reasons for the closing down of profitable firms (Wasserman, 2012). Sometimes the firm gets restarted in another name with another configuration of some of the founders engaging in the restart. The original firm still gets counted as an exit in the data. Additionally, sometimes investors can force firm exit when they determine the need to pull out capital or break up a profitable firm for liquidity reasons (Wasserman, 2003).

That still leaves two kinds of involuntary exits. Sometimes firms simply abort because of a lack of demand and/or run out of cash. Alternatively, firms can go bankrupt with money still owed to creditors (Lawless & Warren, 2005). In addition to a paucity of demand or capital, bankruptcies can ensue internally through mismanagement or externally due to shocks such as a new disruptive technology or regulatory changes.

In sum, the popular press overemphasizes the patently false claim that nine out of ten ventures fail. This number is true for firms funded by venture capitalists. However, venture capital funds less than one-hundredth of 1 percent of firms in the US and even lower fractions in other countries. Strictly speaking, the reverse is true when it comes to the statistics of firm failure (Lawless & Warren, 2005). Only one out of ten firms is clearly a failure, with bankruptcies and money still owed to creditors.

In terms of exits more generally, voluntary and involuntary exits together account for about half of all firms in the economy. Add to that the fact that about a third of exiting firms are profitable at the time of exit, and the landscape of entrepreneurial performance looks very different from received wisdom (Gompers et al., 2006).

Now that we have a clearer picture of success/failure rates of firms, we need to examine an additional confusion that plagues the domain of entrepreneurship. This confusion occurs when the performance of ventures is routinely assumed to be the same as the performance of entrepreneurs. Effectuation consists of lessons entrepreneurs learn through at least ten or more years of immersive experience starting and running multiple firms. Expert entrepreneurs, therefore, learn to take an instrumental view of firm performance. They realize that no matter what the true rate of firm failure may be, they can control and create their own success simply by starting more than one firm. Additionally, as they learn to invest no more than what they can afford to lose in any given venture, they are able to start several. Finally, by making sure they learn and accumulate lessons for each venture and strengthen relationships with stakeholders through multiple projects and ventures, they can cocreate success that leverages failures along the way (Nahata, 2019; Nielsen & Sarasvathy, 2016; Parker, 2013). This is a story not of persistence per se but of building and employing techniques of outliving small failures and cumulating small successes over time.

The right-hand side of Figure 6 illustrates the relationship between the success of a venture and the lessons learned by expert entrepreneurs over time and experience, including multiple ventures. Novice entrepreneurs may start with any mix of prediction and control in their decision and action logics. Preferences for effectual action could be innate in some (rare) cases, but lack of resources may drive people to use effectuation principles such as "bird-in-hand" and "affordable loss," even when their natural inclinations are visionary, adaptive, or causal. However, through multiple ventures or projects within ventures, some of which may fail or succeed, entrepreneurs who continue through to expertise learn the principles of effectuation.

In contrast, most ventures that survive and start growing require some mix and match of both predictive and non-predictive strategies. A large proportion of entrepreneurs either do not want to or are incapable of mixing and matching strategies. Hence, they either quit the venture as it grows beyond a certain stage (mostly to start other new ventures or pursue other careers) or get fired by venture capitalists.

This explains both how expert entrepreneurs become more effectual and why large companies often do not continue to be run by their founders.

A final consideration for understanding the performance implications of effectuation involves the issue of involuntary exit due to external shocks. Both predictive and effectual approaches may be impacted by external shocks entirely out of the control of entrepreneurs. In the predictive case, the predictions could simply be wrong or falsified through external shocks. Similarly, in the effectual case, the venture could run out of the affordable loss limits of its stakeholder commitments, or these commitments could be destroyed through external shocks. In both cases, the venture could be severely or fatally damaged.

To see the overall implications for success and failure in effectuation, we revisit the effectual process in Figure 7.

The important consequences for performance in the effectual process are more interesting than the obvious ones, increasing the probability of success or reducing the probability of failure. Instead, the costs of failure are likely to be lower in the effectual case since no one in the process invests more than they can afford to lose. In other words, irrespective of whether effectuation alters any objective probability of failure that may exist, it reduces the cost of failure nonetheless. Similarly, if and when success does occur, effectuation increases the probability of innovation, especially through the incorporation of self-selected stakeholders, none of whom needs to be prescient or brilliant in their innovative proclivities.

Most importantly, both failures and successes are inputs into the effectual process, not zero-sum outcomes. In terms of outcomes, the process either aborts due to conscious quitting (due to running out of affordable loss resources or

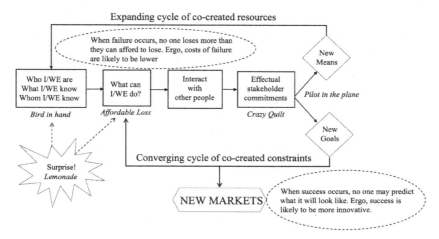

Figure 7 The effectual process with performance implications
(within dashed circles)

conflicts between particular stakeholders) or it results in the cocreation of new markets and other innovative artifacts.

2.6 Finding and Making

Making is very different from finding. And making effectually is very different from making ecologically. The difference hinges on human agency. There is a tendency and a temptation to keep agentic human action out of our theories and models. That is the appeal of the exogenously given scissors of demand and supply in economics. That too is the seduction of some evolutionary and eco-logical models that attribute innovations to blind variation and natural selection, without involving the messiness of human motivations and intersubjective inter-actions such as conversations, commitments, and conflicts. An effectual approach offers practicable heuristics to move about and reshape the prediction-control space while unapologetically embracing William James' (1916) insight, "The trail of the human serpent is over everything."

Traditionally, both ordinary and innovative decisions and behaviors have been modeled in terms of search and selection processes. Whether considered in terms of optimal search, evolutionary models, or complexity landscapes, strategic manage-ment abounds with theories involving search and selection (Angus, 2019; Makadok & Walker, 1996; Posen et al., 2018). In entrepreneurship research, search models are complemented with or sometimes contrasted with models of creation. Recent discussions about the discovery and creation of opportunities offer a case in point (Alvarez & Barney, 2007; Davidsson, 2023; Klein, 2008). These also hark back to Schumpeter's ideas about creative destruction and Hayek's arguments for compe-tition as a discovery procedure. Given that the words "discovery" and "creation" have not only been imbued with multiple and muddled meanings but also evoke specters of debates between science and religion, I wish to use the simpler, more mundane notions of finding and making in this section.

Finding takes the world as given and is largely exogenous to action. Making explicitly emphasizes the endogeneity of the environment to action. Both finding and making rely on prior knowledge. However, whereas finding points to the feasibility of prediction and estimation about the future, making highlights ignorance and unpredictability. Additionally, while finding assumes a sharp sep-aration between the environment and the processes of search, making emphasizes actionable levers for transforming environments and shaping new futures.

2.6.1 Finding and Making Opportunities

The concept of opportunities is important both for entrepreneurship and innov-ation. Casson (1982) defined entrepreneurial opportunities as "situations in which new goods, services, raw materials, and organization methods can be introduced and sold at greater than their cost of production." Entrepreneurs and scholars alike have often assumed that opportunities exist before entrepreneurs take action. They are necessary conditions for entrepreneurship to happen. Shane (2003) argued that opportunities come from technological, political/ regulatory, and social/demographic changes. They could also arise in an idiosyncratic way, out of the errors and omissions of prior decision-makers. Such errors cause surpluses and shortages in the marketplace that offer opportunities entrepreneurs can act on.

As we have seen throughout this Element, entrepreneurs not only find opportunities that arise from these sources but also create them through the effectual process. In other words, opportunities are made as well as found. And as empirical evidence shows, opportunities are perhaps as much the outcomes of what entrepreneurs do as the data based on which they act. We can easily see this if we ask ourselves, "*How* do people become entrepreneurs?" instead of the more traditional question, "Why do some people become entrepreneurs, while others do not?" or its corollary, "Why do some perceive entrepreneurial opportunities and act upon them, when others do not?"

Habitual Entrepreneurship

Some people, whose parents are entrepreneurs, decide either to carry on with the family business or become entrepreneurs in their own right. This is in line with any other profession and tends to be more pronounced in more traditional societies where there is a distinct merchant/business caste or class. In today's world, even children of non-entrepreneurs become entrepreneurs because of early experiences such as a successful newspaper route (Joe O'Donnell, founder of Boston Concessions) or a business selling garbage bags door-to-door as a twelve-year-old (Mark Cuban, founder of Broadcast.com and owner of the Dallas Mavericks).

Necessity Entrepreneurship

There exist a variety of trade-offs between the labor market and entrepreneurial ventures. People get fired from their jobs and become entrepreneurs, or they quit their jobs because the parent company decided not to commercialize their ideas and inventions. Some people are simply unhireable, say, due to lack of education and language skills (immigrant entrepreneurs, for example), or criminal backgrounds (drug lords and protection racketeers, for example), and so become entrepreneurs. In fact, in many parts of the world, even today, steady jobs with large organizations are simply not available, hence necessitating necessity entrepreneurship. Even in OECD countries such as Germany, about

20 percent of entrepreneurs are necessity entrepreneurs, while in developing countries, the proportion may go up above 50 percent (Poschke, 2013).

Incentivized Entrepreneurship

Sometimes, individuals are induced to become entrepreneurs. Governments in almost every country today offer seed money and other incentives to encourage local citizens to start firms and commercialize government-owned technologies (e.g., Battelle National Labs' Entrepreneurial Leave Program). Microfinance organizations, as well as nonprofit international aid organizations (both governmental and nongovernmental), also cajole and/or strong-arm a variety of citizens in many developing countries to start ventures or become self-employed. Increasingly, business schools offer entrepreneurship as a career choice, collaborating with and even cofounding incubators for which they provide a steady pipeline of new entrepreneurs.

Celebrity Entrepreneurship

Some individuals are fortunate enough to experience extraordinary success in their chosen professions. They then decide to found for-profit or nonprofit organizations to create pathways for the less fortunate to find their way to financial independence. Examples abound from show business (Jodie Foster's Egg Pictures, Newman's Own sauces), professional sports (Magic Johnson's theaters), and other areas of the limelight (Oprah Winfrey's plethora of initiatives).

Social Entrepreneurship

People who face extraordinary misfortunes also become entrepreneurs. Some social entrepreneurs, such as Candy Lightner, who founded Mothers Against Drunk Driving after losing her child in a DUI accident, and Sharon Daugherty, founder of Innermotion, who uses dance to rehabilitate victims of sexual abuse, are cases in point. Other social entrepreneurs, like Peter Cove, who founded the for-profit firm America Works to move welfare recipients into the workforce, also attest to the fact that entrepreneurship (for-profit, nonprofit, or hybrid) is an effective way to solve problems in society. Ashoka, a foundation set up by Bill Drayton, offers fellowships for thousands of social entrepreneurs around the world. This permits them to earn a decent wage while leaving a paid job to work full-time on their burgeoning social ventures.

Hybrid Entrepreneurship

A phenomenon of recent interest to entrepreneurship researchers consists in the finding that a sizable proportion of ventures are founded by people who concurrently engage in wage jobs and venturing (Folta et al., 2010). Some estimate that people simultaneously involved in self-employment and wage work may be larger than full-time entrepreneurs (Burke, FitzRoy, & Nolan, 2008). In some of these cases, entrepreneurship is a side hustle. In others, wage employment is simply a way to subsidize and enable entrepreneurship, with the latter being the real focus.

Informal Entrepreneurship

There is a wide variety of ventures also to be found in the "informal" sector of economies. The term informal refers to a wide range of economic transactions that occur outside familiar settings, such as banks and registered companies and organizations. Everything from illegal enterprises, such as drug dealerships, to social entrepreneurs providing much-needed services to people in remote areas where formal recordkeeping is difficult to maintain, tends to be subsumed under the rubric of the informal economy. But it is important to note that the informal sector is not limited to developing countries or nasty illegal activities. Informal ventures proliferate within developed countries and often provide access to vital services to marginalized populations within these countries (Welter et al., 2015). In a recent study of a rural location in the West of the UK, Williams & Nadin (2013) identified and interviewed over 120 informal (i.e., unregistered) entrepreneurial endeavors that provided both for-profit and nonprofit or social goods and services.

Accidental Entrepreneurship

Finally, as already discussed in the earlier section on the downside of opportunities, sometimes entrepreneurship happens entirely accidentally, as in cases involving users and open innovation (Eftekhari & Bores, 2015; Nambisan et al., 2018; Shah & Tripsas, 2007).

In sum, as Aldrich and Ruef (2018) argue, entrepreneurship has misplaced its focus on high-growth firms and heroic entrepreneurs who actually occupy a tiny sliver in one of the tails of the distribution of ventures and entrepreneurs in the real world. This empirical obsession with "black swans" (Taleb 2007) may be academically interesting but is not useful in practice to actual entrepreneurs building real ventures. Furthermore, when we use criteria such as high growth and disruptive novelty in evaluating what counts as an opportunity, this can end up discouraging entrepreneurship. Not only does starting a venture feel like a rash bet or a fool's errand, but it also seems to call for heroic traits that most people understandably feel they do not possess. However, by clearly observing how ventures actually get started and built, we learn that ordinary actionable steps can suffice in people finding and making opportunities.

Several conceptual and empirical developments in a variety of disciplines speak to this understanding of effectual cocreation. In the ensuing subsections, I provide a very quick and impressionistic summary of ideas from the disciplines that make the case on both sides of the finding and making worldviews. The key point to note here is not whether one is right or wrong, nor even which one may be more or less useful from any given disciplinary lens, but to clearly show that there is room in every discipline for ways to make new worlds and futures, not only take them as completely exogenous to human action. It is further important to note that the endogeneity goes in both directions, from making to finding and back to making.

2.6.2 Philosophy

Philosophers have examined how means and ends may be shaped and formed through creative human action. Hans Joas explored this through ideas about ends-in-view from John Dewey (Joas, 1996). In *Pragmatism,* according to Goodman (2021), William James "holds neither that we create our truths out of nothing, nor that truth is entirely independent of humanity. He embraces "the humanistic principle: you can't weed out the human contribution" (p. 122). He also embraces a metaphysics of process in the claim that "for pragmatism [reality] is still in the making," whereas for "rationalism reality is ready-made and complete from all eternity" (p. 123).

The philosopher of mind, Nelson Goodman (1983) argued from the problem of induction that we need to rethink the very conceptualization of the universe of all possible worlds. He urges instead (to repeat the quote at the beginning of this section): *We have come to think of the actual as one of all possible worlds. We need to repaint that picture. All possible worlds lie within the actual one.*

We don't need to contest the ontological truth of these claims in order to see that whether we engage with environments and futures as shapeable or not influences the actions we take and the choices we make. The psychology of making is, in itself, a powerful thing, irrespective of our philosophical or ideological positions on whether reality is in the making or whether our actions are overdetermined by our circumstances.

2.6.3 Psychology

At face value, the psychology of making turns our attention to what is immediately controllable and what may be perceived as less malleable. Take the case of personality, for example. Traits, by definition, are aspects of the psyche that are not easily changeable in the short run. Over the history of psychology, theorists have differed in how rigid or hardwired they have deemed personality (Buss, 1989; McAdams & Olson, 2010).

Age-old debates have tried to parse the differential effects of nature versus nurture. Recently, the conversation has moved to lay theories about whether abilities such as intelligence are deemed as fixed inborn traits or whether they are seen as changeable or shapeable through education and other interventions. Accumulating evidence supports the latter view (Gopnik, 1992; Molden & Dweck, 2006; Murphy & Dweck, 2010). The conversation has moved to more complex multifactorial approaches to interactions between the two (Hambrick et al., 2018; Keller, 2010). Similar developments can be found in literature examining the role of genotypes and phenotypes (Kamat et al., 2019). The rise in understanding of genetics also ushered in an era of epigenetics (Cavalli & Heard, 2019).

Recent advances in the brain sciences have for a while argued for the changeability of the brain during developmental years, early childhood, and adolescence, for example. Theories have suggested that the brain could not grow neurons later in life. The ability to learn a new language and speak it in flawless native accents has often been touted as proof of this idea. However, a deeper look at neuroplasticity yielded surprising evidence for the brain to change itself even later in life (Lillard & Erisir, 2011; Shaffer, 2012). Currently, the conversation has moved to the question of the balance between plasticity and stability. Studies seek to tease out the nuances about how much of each, when, and under what conditions (Yin & Yuan, 2015). The concept of critical development windows, as well as interventions to tweak plasticity, is beginning to emerge in the field.

In decision theory, where formal models dominate, little progress has been possible beyond search and selection models. However, even in mathematical formulations, there are new developments such as the "do" calculus developed by Judea Pearl (Pearl, 2009). Developments in logic, such as mereology (Varzi, 2019) and relevance logic (Dunn & Restall, 2002), also offer tools to tackle endogeneities between actions within one's control and distributions exogenously given. I have developed elsewhere the idea that expert entrepreneurs do Bayesianism differently (Sarasvathy, Menon, & Kuechle, 2013). Instead of using observations to update prior beliefs (instance of finding), they look for conditioning assumptions that they can reify or falsify through means within their control (instance of making).

Finally, work related to the development of expertise in cognitive science embraces the view that deliberate practice and long-term immersive experiences can speed up pattern recognition, even in complex domains (Ericsson, 2006). This speeding up literally rewires the brain, transforming novices into experts. In this sense, not only the world but also the person acting on and interacting with it can be "made," not only found.

2.6.4 Sociology

This understanding of the making of persons is visible in sociological theories about how structure constrains and shapes agency. Starting with the works of Durkheim (culture is determined by social structure) and Simmel (formal properties of social structure condition all kinds of behaviors), sociologists have argued that the primacy of structure is the distinguishing characteristic of sociological and anthropological explanations. Otherwise, these would collapse into psychology or economics. As Black (2000, p. 705) put it, *Pure sociology implies the presence of several absences: ideology, teleology, psychology, and people.*

Currently, structural approaches can be found in the literature on social networks, for instance, in the seminal works of Ronald Burt (1982) and in institutional theories inspired by Parsons and Merton (Scott, 2005). Interestingly, we also find rising interest in institutional entrepreneurship, where agency plays a stronger role in overcoming institutional inertia to modify structure (Leca, Battilana, & Boxenbaum, 2008). This stream builds on contemporary sociologists such as Bourdieu and Giddens, who have softened the strong stance of structural views of sociology by creating spaces for individual and group action to at least alternate and iterate with structural influences (Sarason, Dean, & Dillard, 2006).

In the tradition of Mead and others is the social philosopher I mentioned earlier, Hans Joas, a strong proponent for the role of creative action (Joas, 1996). Joas emphasizes corporeality, sociality, and situation in conjunction with creative action at the individual and group levels to offer a sociological approach that coheres well with the effectual process.

Several of these strands from philosophy, psychology, and sociology that offer spaces for the effectual worldview to manifest in human action come together in empirical precision in studies of interaction in social psychology.

2.6.5 Social Psychology

In contrast to the reflexive influences of structure and agency on each other, as conceptualized by sociologists, or the restriction of our understanding of behavior to what goes on in individual brains, as in psychology, the view from social psychology builds on individual variation, even in the face of the exact same situation. Furthermore, it treats interactions between individuals as primitive to the transformation of structure.

The renowned social psychologist Harold Kelley defined interaction as a transformative phenomenon as follows (Kelley, 2000): "In the transformation model, we implicitly use a simple expansion of Lewin's famous formula that behavior is a function of the environment and the person. Specifically, we assume that interaction is a joint function of the given situation and the two persons, A & B" (Kelley, 2000: 7).

This definition draws upon an important insight: "The transformation process is a theoretical way to account for the obvious fact–undoubtedly part of common sense–*that for a particular "given" situation, different people make different things out of it*" (Kelley, 2000: 6) (Italics in original).

Thus, social psychology embraces "making" as fundamental. No situation, even the most mundane, is simply "found" when two individuals are present in it. The trail of the human serpent, as William James explained, is indeed over everything.

Over decades of empirical studies, social psychologists and game theorists have collected and taxonomized transformative interactional situations into atlases, games, and institutional building blocks. Each of these offers the groundwork on which studies of effectual entrepreneurial making can be formulated and understood. And the artifacts of such making form the primitives of economics that we take for granted: supply, demand, and the price mechanism.

2.6.6 Economics

The standard model of the basic framework of market economics is inspired by physics and incorporated into notions of equilibrium. The model begins with certain axiomatic assumptions about the behavior at the micro-level that, through the process of equilibration, results in outcomes at the macro-level that can be formally shown to be beneficial in various ways (Varian, 2014).

Simply put, individuals (and firms) have clear, well-ordered preferences that can be aggregated into utility functions. These form the supply and demand schedules for suppliers and consumers of any given product. The simple mechanics of market exchange, modeled in terms of movements in price and quantity, can thereafter lead to an optimum level of satisfaction for both suppliers and consumers in the market. Additionally, these equilibrium arrangements add up to a Pareto-optimal economy in which we can rest assured, at least, that no one will be worse off. Finally, this system does not require intervention from any central authority, human or divine.

This powerful formal model, encapsulated in countless institutional struggles throughout history and across different countries and cultures, has come to dominate not only economic theory but also the reality of institutions around the world today. Yet, throughout this history, and especially today, profound discomforts with the model also proliferate. The strongest rivalry to market economics came from Marxist assaults (Marx, 1867; McNally, 1993). Skousen (2015) succinctly captures the contrast between Adam Smith and Karl Marx: "If the work of Adam Smith is the Genesis of modern economics, that of Karl Marx is its Exodus. If the Scottish philosopher is the great creator of laissez-faire, the German revolutionary is its great destroyer." As Skousen goes on to point out, "Marxist John E. Roemer admits as much." What Roemer (1988) admits to is that while Smith saw benevolence in self-interest and creativity in competition, Marx perceived class struggles and anarchy in the former and a pulverizing iron fist in the latter.

Yet, both free market and Marxist economics could not find a role for the entrepreneur. The former models managers and entrepreneurs as mere calculators seeking to solve an optimization problem involving profit maximization as an objective function constrained by a small set of rather well-defined decision variables such as price, output, marketing budgets, and technological trajectories. Marx, as Hebert and Link (2007) point out, "treated both capitalists and entrepreneurs with disdain." Even in approaches that allow for something more than profit maximization, such as Williamson's (1963) theory of managerial discretion or Schumpeter's (1942) theory of creative destruction, the role of the entrepreneur equates to thin descriptions. Discretion involves maximizing something other than profit, and creative destruction mostly refers to combinatorial innovations changing the competitive landscape and eventually leading to the routinization of innovative activity within large bureaucratic firms, obviating the need for the entrepreneur. Neither undertakes a deeper dive into what entrepreneurs actually do. Baumol provocatively summarized the nonexistence of entrepreneurship in economics as follows: " . . . the Prince of Denmark has been expunged from the discussion of *Hamlet*" (Baumol, 1968, p. 66).

This is indeed a puzzle. Why would economic theorists have such difficulty including entrepreneurship? One answer to the puzzle is the influence of physics. The natural sciences cannot deal with teleology. Different sciences can tackle material, efficient, and formal causation to greater or lesser degrees, but the natural sciences explicitly eschew concepts like intentions and purposes. As we saw in the foregoing summaries, even the social sciences treat these either as unexplained primitives to behavior or artifacts of physical or structural processes in the body, brain, society, and culture. In other words, the physics-inspired standard economic model cannot handle the construction of preferences or the cocreation of markets.

Recently, models inspired by biology, whether evolutionary or ecological, have sought to modify the standard model. However, these models take variations in human behavior as random inputs into the system. No explanations are provided as to how preferences and goals may come to be. Even in psychological studies focused on goal-related behavior, the origins of goals remain unexplained. Consider statements from prominent scholars in the area: "Goals come into their models as a deus ex machina, something that needs no explanation" (Csikszentmihalyi & Nakamura, 1999). "Although reasonable, the notion that people set their own goals raises the intriguing question how they do this" (Aarts, 2019, p. 106).

Effectual behavior suggests the beginnings of an explanation for goal cocreation that can precede explanations of economic behavior and even the behavior of markets and governments.

2.6.7 Political Economy

By markets, I refer to an economic organization built on free exchange between buyers and sellers. By government, I mean a centralized or hierarchical political organization imbued with coercive authority to collect taxes and enforce regulations. In the ensuing discussion, I don't see the two as entirely independent or mutually exclusive. To function well, markets require certain regulatory guardrails. Similarly, governments require freely functioning markets to fund a viable system of law and order. Yet, these two are distinct in ways that matter. Moreover, these two distinct ways of organizing human activity constrain and bound the prediction-control space. At the same time, as effectuators navigate and reshape the space, their actions also impinge on these boundaries.

Some entrepreneurial actions may explicitly seek to reshape the boundaries between markets and governments. Private military contractors in the US are a case in point. Others may produce innovations that inadvertently disturb existing boundaries, requiring new regulations to be enacted and enforced, or old regulations to be retired. Examples of these include artificial intelligence and social media. Yet others offer opportunities for productive new public–private partnerships. The development of COVID-19 vaccines provides recent examples. Additionally, "social entrepreneurship" is a rising new field of activity and research. Social ventures seek to solve large complex social problems using practices and techniques from private enterprise. Consider examples such as Grameen Bank tackling poverty or Transparency International taking on corruption. Crises such as climate change are accelerating social entrepreneurship in domains ranging from the commercialization of renewable energy to the rehabilitation of migrants and rebuilding of disaster zones.

In other words, entrepreneurs are increasingly involved not only in building familiar for-profit firms but also in building new institutions and organizations that defy conventional notions of "firms," "markets," and "governments." Therefore, it would be worth exploring how an effectual view can help us rethink taken-for-granted assumptions about the relative roles of markets and governments in the political economy.

In this connection, two related concepts from economics are worth examining in more detail. The first one is "market failure" which may be more familiar than the second one, "polycentric governance," that comes from the work of Nobel laureate Elinor Ostrom (2010). Both terms begin with the idea that while certain governmental regulations are required for markets to function well, markets, when they do function well, provide the most efficient form of economic organization. However, when they don't function well, we encounter "market failure."

An iconic example of market failure is the "tragedy of the commons" (Hardin, 1968) where some resources (such as clean air) are free to everyone in a community. Such common pool resources require the community to nurture and manage them. However, since they cannot be broken up into private property, there is no incentive for any member of the community to incur the costs of taking care of them. In these cases of market failure, governments need to step in and take action. Or some other form of "collective action" (such as trade unions) becomes necessary (Olson, 1971).

Ostrom's argument is theoretical, albeit a compelling one. Ostrom invested decades of research into the histories of several such situations of market failure to show how small groups of individuals came together to manage them without necessitating governmental action. From the vast amounts of in-depth data from around the world, she chronicled a process called the Institutional Analysis and Development (IAD) framework that explains the development of "polycentric governance" mechanisms. These mechanisms do not fit into the institutional structure of centralized governments, whether local or national. They also transcend market transactions. Instead, they rearrange the boundaries between market structures and government structures, enabling new kinds of institutions to be cocreated. In a recent article, we reanalyzed Ostrom's data on the allocation of water rights in the Los Angeles basins in the 1930s to show exactly how an effectual process drives the heart of Ostrom's IAD framework (Sarasvathy & Ramesh, 2019).

In particular, the effectual process at the heart of the IAD framework explains how both clear and ambiguous goals of individuals get reshaped into the cocreation of the new polycentric governance mechanisms. This allows us to extend the cocreation of new ends worth achieving to the level of a community as a whole. Just as studies of goals in psychology have not paid attention to where goals come from in the first place, current debates about the role of markets versus governments assume developmental and environmental goals as given and even obvious (Mazzucato, 2015; Moyo, 2009). In a characteristically complex yet insightful analysis titled *Development as Freedom*, Amartya Sen urges us not to treat the poor and unfortunate as patients (Sen, 1999). Instead, he argues that economic development should treat people as active agents shaping their own ends. His work has inspired the formulation of the Human Development Index that measures capabilities, not only outcomes such as GDP and PCI (Anand & Sen, 1994).

If we are to build on the works of economists such as Ostrom and Sen to help entrepreneurs develop ventures that effectively reshape the boundaries between markets and governments, we need to understand the conditions under which effectuation can drive the cocreation of public–private partnerships, as well as new organizations and institutions of polycentric governance. Figure 8 provides a framework for the role of effectual entrepreneurship when market failures occur under conditions of Knightian uncertainty.

Figure 8 illustrates how effectual entrepreneurs can get going under Knightian uncertainty to help cocreate new structures for navigating the boundaries between markets and governments, whether in terms of capital allocation or collective action (Sarasvathy, 2021). The left-hand sides of Figures 8a and 8b depict the traditional view of markets and governments. In this view, government action is seen as the remedy for market failures. The view from effectuation shows that entrepreneurs can and do help shape and cocreate new markets. Additionally, they can also move the boundaries between markets and governments, especially under conditions of uncertainty where both market action and government action might have trouble getting a kick start.

The right-hand sides in Figure 8 offer at least two examples of when and how an effectual approach could get the ball rolling. Figure 8a shows the case where large capital allocations, much beyond the coffers of individual investors and private syndicates, may be called for to overcome market failure. The right-hand side of Figure 8b illustrates situations requiring more than funding, such as those involving collective action where individuals lack incentives to act on their own.

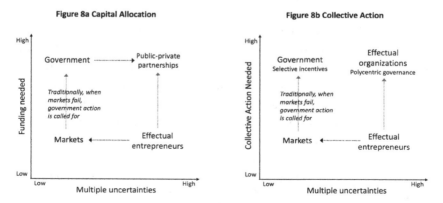

Figure 8 Markets, governments, and effectual entrepreneurship under uncertainty

In further explicating the framework in Figure 8, however, I will eschew the term "market failure" since it sets up a false dichotomy between markets and governments, which I already repudiated at the beginning of this section.

The intuition for Figure 8a is that when funding requirements are very large, states will have a larger role to play, even though they may need to be cajoled into it through effectual action under uncertainty. Renewable energy companies collaborating with state investments in R&D is a case in point. The intuition for Figure 8b has to do with the argument from the literature on collective action for the need for selective incentives to induce individuals to contribute to the common good. Take the case of COVID-19 vaccination. While some people unhesitatingly volunteer to get vaccinated, others refuse or hesitate for a variety of different reasons. Yet the benefits of vaccination depend on almost everyone in the population getting vaccinated. Therefore, selective incentives have to be developed and implemented to get everyone vaccinated.

Incentives required may be large or small, depending on specific situations. Governments can provide both positive and negative incentives, but only in situations where the consequences are highly predictable, as in the case of the COVID vaccine. However, it is harder, if not impossible, for governments to enact and implement incentives in situations of Knightian uncertainty. Issues related to climate change are a case in point here. In such cases, the type of effectual collective action, as we saw in the LA water rights case, becomes necessary and useful. Furthermore, this effectual action can move from the effectual quadrant in Figure 8 toward public–private partnerships or even result in innovative new polycentric governance institutions that can straddle and reshape the boundaries between markets and governments.

Effectual actions and interactions in the prediction-control space are not limited to firms and markets. They can help remake the worlds we live in.

In sum,

Worlds can be made. Futures can be made. But they are not made from nothing. And they are not simply made as imagined. The constraints of means currently under control are real. They are not changeable through individual wishful thinking or will, however powerfully and persuasively imagined. Instead, flexibility in goals can be the most useful tool in making the world anew, especially in opening the door to self-selection by stakeholders willing to make valuable commitments. Both clear, well-ordered preferences and inchoate aspirations are ingredients facilitating the molding of these new goals that are themselves cocreated through the effectual process. Without goal ambiguity, worldmaking can become a difficult and stultifying endeavor surrendering agency to tyranny of various kinds, while also getting battered by the vagaries of Knightian uncertainty.

The fact that every one of the social sciences has, however recently and reluctantly, found a space for making brings us to the most important artifact that the effectual process can make: the cocreation of purpose itself.

"There is no end / To what a living world / Will demand of you." *Octavia E. Butler, Parable of the Sower, Earthseed Series* (Butler, 2012)

3 Predictive Science and Effectual Entrepreneurship

Issues related to value have traditionally been assigned to the domain of ethics, whether in religious or secular terms. Another way to think about value is in terms of truth, beauty, and goodness, with truth inhabiting science, beauty inhabiting art, and goodness inhabiting ethics. However, we continually redraw the boundaries of these. Domains such as technology, philosophy, and the social sciences often traverse these domains and trample their boundaries. Psychology and economics have, in recent times, embraced happiness and well-being as legitimate dependent variables. Similarly, beauty and art have been brought into the purview of technology and vice versa. Mind, matter, and mathematics are up for grabs not only in philosophy but also in the psychologist's lab, the physicist's colliders, and in the intelligence of machines, embodied and otherwise. Perhaps the boundaries were always more permeable than our categories might surmise. In the meantime, for the most part, the scientific method gains ground over all of these. Hopefully. I, for one, am thankful for that.

Prediction is the touchstone of the scientific method. Theories are considered scientific to the extent that they can make predictions that can, at least in principle, be tested through careful, reliable, replicable empirical observations, whether in the lab or in the world. Hence the exhortation to formulate theories as falsifiable hypotheses. While making can be a part of science, the ultimate objective is to move toward finding testable predictions about what exists, and how exactly.

Tested and testable predictions form the bulk of scientific knowledge. Ideally, to know something or to achieve predictive control, we need to be able to find conditions that are both necessary and sufficient. In cases where this is difficult or impossible, at the very least, we still look for necessary, even if insufficient, conditions. Effectuation, in contrast, builds on sufficient conditions, each of which may be unnecessary. This allows the effectual process to operate even in the absence of predictable knowledge. Just working with sufficiency, without necessity, the effectual process allows the making of things, including the building blocks of science, be it the formulation of new hypotheses or the design of experiments. Experiential interactions with the physical and social world are as important ingredients to these as knowledge accumulated through falsified predictions.

Making something based on science or anything else within our control is the realm of design. Design can take the form of engineering or art or anything that we choose to make, with or without the knowledge acquired through science. Simon thus distinguished the natural and social sciences from design by postulating the sciences of the artificial (Simon, 1996). I have argued elsewhere that entrepreneurship is a science of the artificial in the Simonian sense.

In fact, I conceptualize entrepreneurship as something larger: a method that complements but is distinguishable from the scientific method (Sarasvathy & Venkataraman, 2011). And just as the notion of experimentation is at the heart of the scientific method, I posit effectuation at the heart of the entrepreneurial method. Predictive control is the holy grail of the scientific method, while non-predictive control drives the entrepreneurial method.

The source of this intuition comes from a simple logical dichotomy. Either effectuation is an important idea capable of making an actual difference in the world and enduring over time. Or not. If it is not, my intuition will easily be dissolved soon enough. If it is, it would surely be worth investigating its role in shaping artifacts beyond a narrowly defined realm of starting and running firms.

One way to interrogate this intuition is to empirically examine it in phenomena beyond familiar notions of entrepreneurship. Specifically, it should be possible to uncover the principles and process of effectuation in data collected for other purposes. In one such study, we reanalyzed Elinor Ostrom's historical case study of the allocation of water rights in the Los Angeles basin in the early twentieth-century America. We not only uncovered evidence for the process of effectuation but were also able to theoretically embed it within the IAD framework that Ostrom and her colleagues had developed to study instances of polycentric governance around the world (Sarasvathy & Ramesh, 2019).

Other studies that have examined effectuation in settings outside of entrepreneurship include the cocreation of cubism by Picasso and Braque (Olive-Tomas & Harmeling, 2020) and the use of effectuation in the Toquaht nation in Canada (Murphy, Danis, & Mack, 2020). This broadening of the effectual horizon has strengthened my intuition of how effectuation could propel something as large as a method complementing the reach of the scientific method.

Given a goal, something worth pursuing, experimentation in science offers the gold standard for how to pursue it. Effectual entrepreneurship concerns itself with a method to cocreate new goals, to shape what is worth pursuing next.

We can and have put the scientific method to work on problems we want to solve and goals we want to achieve. For example, finding a vaccine for COVID-19. However, getting the vaccine into the arms of people is a task that requires the entrepreneurial method. We cannot simply rest on the assumption that once the vaccine is available, people will predictably turn up with their sleeves rolled up for the jab, or that politics and regulations can get the job done. Techniques of persuasion, bargaining, cajoling, coercing, and cocreating have to be devised, whether at the level of individuals or groups. Not only judgments but actual transformations of market mechanisms and state apparatus, as well as the redesign of public–private partnerships, need to be added to the task list. In this space, the principles and process of effectuation can do really useful work.

The case of the vaccine illustrates how the two methods can work in domains where the goal is specific and given – namely, invent a vaccine and vaccinate the entire population. How about in cases where it is not clear which goals are worth pursuing? Or goals that are still in-the-making or yet-to-be-made?

As science moves outward, the frontiers of current knowledge and increases the circumference of the predictable, it also expands the set of possible goals to choose from. These new goals may be intended outcomes or unintended side effects of the scientific method in action. Harking back to the COVID vaccine, the introduction of a new kind of vaccine based on mRNA opens the door not only to speedier vaccines and therapeutics in the future but also to new bio-engineering possibilities, some of which simply cannot be predicted ex ante. As John Cooke, the medical director of the RNA Therapeutics Program at the Houston Methodist Research Institute, observed, "It's essentially biological software."

The entrepreneurial method can help shape choices about which of these new possibilities are pursued and how we can embody them in new goals not yet imagined. Notice that the claim here goes beyond normative aspects of which goals currently predictable should or should not be pursued. The entrepreneurial method can be used both by good and bad actors, just as the scientific method can be. "Bad" scientists can help engineer viruses that "bad" entrepreneurs can then use in bioterrorism. Yet, most "good" science requires cooperation across large networks of scientists, laboratories, and universities. This, in turn, calls for regulatory and self-regulatory mechanisms within the system that increase the likelihood that good science will proliferate, dominate, mitigate, and marginal-ize bad science. Similarly, we need to build systems and infrastructures for the entrepreneurial method that allow more and more people to be involved in effectuating new purposes that propel us outward while keeping torpedo risks within affordable loss levels.

Currently, the forging of new goals, such as the United Nations' Sustainable Development Goals, is in the hands of a privileged few, with most of humanity left as unwitting stakeholders who have little control over the process. The notion of worth or value is left either to those with power, fame, or means, or to historical–cultural habits and traditions. Effectuation offers a way to democratize purpose. This is analogous to the democratization of knowledge and income that occurred through the spread of scientific education. Before that, increases in knowledge and income were limited to very few people, estimated by historians at less than 4 percent of the population. By educating and enabling everyone to become effectuators, we can engage more people in the systematic cocreation of a variety of new goals worth achieving while investing no more than we can afford to lose. Some of these will coalesce into valuable new futures we cannot currently predict or even imagine.

Consider the history of human rights. Both words in the phrase "human rights" had to be invented (Hunt, 2007). Yet, these were not inventions attributable to science. For millennia, we lived without a concept of rights, and until recently, rights were not accorded to all humans, not even in principle. Yet somehow, the arc of history has been bent toward a widening of the circle of both what counts as human and what counts as rights. I don't believe there was or is anything inevitable about this curvature. Instead, I hypothesize that the makings of an effectual entrepreneurial method went hand in hand with the bending of that arc. I further conjecture that the effectual entrepreneurial method has to work with the experimental scientific method if we are to build on our successes to date and outlive failures to come.

This conjecture is neither hope nor promise. It simply acknowledges the fact that the bias for effectual action and interaction is rational in the face of true unpredictability. If we venture, we may or may not succeed. But if we don't, we certainly will not.

And even when we do, our venture will entail making new purposes. It stands to reason, then, that the design of the greatest import will entail the design of one's own destiny. And the purpose of freedom will consist in the freedom to shape one's purposes. Let's examine how the ideas in this Element may be of use in this venture, as it has been in the experiences and learnings of expert entrepreneurs.

References

Aarts, H. 2019. Goal setting theory and the mystery of setting goals. *Motivation Science, 5*(2), 106–107.

Allen, P. (2012). *Idea Man: A Memoir by the Cofounder of Microsoft.* New York: Penguin.

Aldrich, H. E., & Ruef, M. (2018). Unicorns, gazelles, and other distractions on the way to understanding real entrepreneurship in the United States. *Academy of Management Perspectives, 32*(4), 458–472.

Alsos, G. A., Clausen, T. H., Hytti, U., & Solvoll, S. (2016). Entrepreneurs' social identity and the preference of causal and effectual behaviours in start-up processes. *Entrepreneurship & Regional Development, 28*(3–4), 234–258.

Alsos, G. A., Clausen, T. H., Mauer, R., Read, S., & Sarasvathy, S. D. (2019). Effectual exchange: From entrepreneurship to the disciplines and beyond. *Small Business Economics, 54*, 605–619.

Alvarez, S. A., & Barney, J. B. (2007). Discovery and creation: Alternative theories of entrepreneurial action. *Strategic Entrepreneurship Journal, 1*(1–2), 11–26.

Amit, R., Muller, E., & Cockburn, I. (1995). Opportunity costs and entrepreneurial activity. *Journal of Business Venturing, 10*(2), 95–106.

Anand, S., & Sen, A. (1994). Human Development Index: Methodology and Measurement. Technical report, Human Development Report Office (HDRO), United Nations Development Programme (UNDP).

Andriani, P., & Cattani, G. (2016). Exaptation as source of creativity, innovation, and diversity: Introduction to the special section. *Industrial and Corporate Change, 25*(1), 115–131.

Andrews, K. R. (1997). The concept of corporate strategy. *Resources, Firms, and Strategies: A Reader in the Resource-Based Perspective, 52*, 11–52.

Angus, R. W. (2019). Problemistic search distance and entrepreneurial performance. *Strategic Management Journal, 40*(12), 2011–2023.

Arrow, K. J., & Debreu, G. (1954). Existence of an equilibrium for a competitive economy. *Econometrica: Journal of the Econometric Society, 22*, 265–290.

Audretsch, D. B., Santarelli, E., & Vivarelli, M. (1999). Start-up size and industrial dynamics: Some evidence from Italian manufacturing. *International Journal of Industrial Organization, 17*(7), 965–983.

Baker, T., & Nelson, R. E. (2005). Creating something from nothing: Resource construction through entrepreneurial bricolage. *Administrative Science Quarterly, 50*(3), 329–366.

Barney, J. (1991). Firm resources and sustained competitive advantage. *Journal of Management, 17*(1), 99–120.

Baumol, W. J. (1968). Entrepreneurship in economic theory. *The American Economic Review*, 58 (2), 64–71.

Beatty, J., & Carrera, I. (2011). When what had to happen was not bound to happen: History, chance, narrative, evolution. *Journal of the Philosophy of History, 5*(3), 471–495.

Bemmaor, A. C. (1995). Predicting behavior from intention-to-buy measures: The parametric case. *Journal of Marketing Research, 32*(2), 176–191.

Black, D. (2000). The purification of sociology. *Contemporary Sociology, 29* (5), 704–709.

Bloemen-Bekx, M., Lambrechts, F., & Van Gils, A. (2021). An exploration of the role of intuitive forms of planning in the succession process: The explanatory power of effectuation theory. *Journal of Family Business Management, 13*(2), 486–502.

Brealey, R., & Myers, S. (1984). *Principles of Corporate Finance*. New York: McGraw-Hill/Irwin

Brettel, M., Mauer, R., Engelen, A., & Küpper, D. (2012). Corporate effectuation: Entrepreneurial action and its impact on R&D project performance. *Journal of Business Venturing, 27*(2), 167–184.

Brockhaus Sr., R. H. (1980). Risk taking propensity of entrepreneurs. *Academy of Management Journal, 23*(3), 509–520.

Bromiley, P., & Curley, S. P. (1992). Individual differences in risk taking. In J. F. Yates (ed.), *Risk-Taking Behavior*, pp. 87–132. John Wiley & Sons.

Burke, A. E., FitzRoy, F. R., & Nolan, M. A. (2008). What makes a die-hard entrepreneur? Beyond the "employee or entrepreneur" dichotomy. *Small Business Economics, 31*, 93–115.

Burt, R. S. (1982). *Toward a Structural Theory of Action* (Vol. 10). New York: Academic Press.

Buss, A. H. (1989). Personality as traits. *American Psychologist, 44*(11), 1378–1388.

Butler, O. E. (2012). *Parable of the Sower* (Vol. 1). New York: Open Road Media.

Camerer, C., & Lovallo, D. (1999). Overconfidence and excess entry: An experimental approach. *American Economic Review, 89*(1), 306–318.

Cardon, M. S., & Kirk, C. P. (2015). Entrepreneurial passion as mediator of the self–efficacy to persistence relationship. *Entrepreneurship Theory and Practice, 39*(5), 1027–1050.

Cassar, G. (2006). Entrepreneur opportunity costs and intended venture growth. *Journal of Business Venturing, 21*(5), 610–632.

Casson, M. (1982). *The entrepreneur: An economic theory.* Rowman & Littlefield.

Cavalli, G., & Heard, E. (2019). Advances in epigenetics link genetics to the environment and disease. *Nature, 571*(7766), 489–499.

Chakrabarty, S., & Erin Bass, A. (2015). Comparing virtue, consequentialist, and deontological ethics-based corporate social responsibility: Mitigating microfinance risk in institutional voids. *Journal of Business Ethics, 126*(3), 487–512.

Chang, E. C., & Pinegar, J. M. (1988). A fundamental study of the seasonal risk-return relationship: A note. *The Journal of Finance, 43*(4), 1035–1039.

Chiappe, D. L., & Kukla, A. (1996). Context selection and the frame problem. *Behavioral and Brain Sciences, 19*(3), 529–530.

Christensen, C. M., Raynor, M., & Verlinden, M. (2001). Skate to where the money will be. *Harvard Business Review, 79*(10), 72–83.

Cohen, A. (2003). *The Perfect Store: Inside eBay.* New York: Back Bay Books.

Corner, P. D., & Ho, M. (2010). How opportunities develop in social entrepreneurship. *Entrepreneurship Theory and Practice, 34*(4), 635–659.

Crisp, R. (2021). Well-being. In E. N. Zalta (Ed.), *The Stanford Encyclopedia of Philosophy* (Vol. Winter 2021). https://plato.stanford.edu/archives/win2021/entries/well-being/

Csikszentmihalyi, M., & Nakamura, J. (1999). Emerging goals and the self-regulation of be- havior. In R. S. Wyer (Ed.), *Advances in Social Cognition: Vol. 12. Perspectives on Behavioral Self-regulation* (pp. 107–118). Mahwah, NJ: Erl- baum.

Cyert, R. M., & March, J. G. (1963/1992). *A Behavioral Theory of the Firm, 2nd ed.* Englewood Cliffs, NJ: Prentice Hall.

Davidsson, P. (2023). Ditching discovery-creation for unified venture creation research. *Entrepreneurship Theory and Practice, 47*(2), 594–612.

Dew, N. (2009). Serendipity in entrepreneurship. *Organization Studies, 30*(7), 735–753.

Dew, N., Ramesh, A., Read, S., Sarasvathy, S. D., & Virginia, V. (2018). Toward deliberate practice in the development of entrepreneurial expertise: The anatomy of the effectual ask. In K. A. Ericsson, R. R. Hoffman, A. Kozbelt, & A. M. Williams (Eds.), *The Cambridge Handbook of*

Expertise and Expert Performance, 389–412. Cambridge: Cambridge University Press.

Dew, N., Sarasathy, S. D., Read, S., & Wiltbank, R. (2009). Affordable loss: Behavioral economic aspects of the plunge decision. *Strategic Entrepreneurship Journal, 3*(2), 105–126.

Dew, N., Sarasvathy, S. D., & Venkataraman, S. (2004). The economic implications of exaptation. *Journal of Evolutionary Economics, 14*(1), 69–84.

Domino, B., & Conway, D. W. (2000). Optimism and pessimism from a historical perspective. In E. C. Chang (Ed.), *Optimism & Pessimism: Implications for Theory, Research, and Practice*, (pp. 3–10). Washington, DC: American Psychological Association.

Dunn, J. M., & Restall, G. (2002). Relevance logic. In Dov M. Gabbay and Franz Guenthner (Eds.), *Handbook of Philosophical Logic* (pp. 1–128). Dordrecht: Kluwer Academic Publishers.

Edwards, W., & Fasolo, B. (2001). Decision technology. *Annual Review of Psychology, 52*(1), 581–606.

Elster, J. (2000). *Ulysses Unbound: Studies in Rationality, Precommitment, and Constraints*. Cambridge: Cambridge University Press.

Ericsson, K. A., Krampe, R. T., & Tesch-Römer, C. (1993). The role of deliberate practice in the acquisition of expert performance. *Psychological Review, 100*(3), 363–406. http://search.epnet.com/direct.asp?an=rev100336 3&db=pdh&tg=AN

Ericsson, K. A., & Simon, H. A. (1993). *Protocol Analysis: Verbal Reports as Data*. Cambridge, MA: MIT Press.

Ericsson, K. A. (2006). The influence of experience and deliberate practice on the development of superior expert performance. In K. A. Ericsson, N. Charness, P. Feltovich, R. R. Hoffman (Eds.), *The Cambridge Handbook of Expertise and Expert Performance*, (pp. 685–706). Cambridge: Cambridge University Press.

Feenstra, R. C., & Hamilton, G. G. (2006). *Emergent Economies, Divergent Paths: Economic Organization and International Trade in South Korea and Taiwan* (Vol. 29). Cambridge: Cambridge University Press.

Feibleman, J. K. (1972). The testing of laws: Prediction and control. In *Scientific Method* (pp. 195–213). Dordrecht: Springer.

Fischer, D., Greven, A., Tornow, M., & Brettel, M. (2021). On the value of effectuation processes for R&D alliances and the moderating role of R&D alliance experience. *Journal of Business Research, 135*, 606–619.

Fischer, E., & Reuber, A. R. (2011). Social interaction via new social media: (How) can interactions on Twitter affect effectual thinking and behavior? *Journal of Business Venturing, 26*(1), 1–18.

Fodor, J. A. (2008). Modularity of mind: An essay on faculty psychology. In J. E. Adler, & L. J. Rips (Eds.), *Reasoning: Studies of Human Inference and Its Foundations* (pp. 878–914). Cambridge: Cambridge University Press. (Reprinted from *Modularity of Mind: An Essay on Faculty Psychology*, 1983, Cambridge, MA: MIT Press.)

Folta, T. B., Delmar, F., & Wennberg, K. (2010). Hybrid entrepreneurship. *Management Science, 56*(2), 253–269.

Frese, T., Geiger, I., & Dost, F. (2020). An empirical investigation of determinants of effectual and causal decision logics in online and high-tech start-up firms. *Small Business Economics, 54*(3), 641–664.

Gabrielsson, J., & Politis, D. (2011). Career motives and entrepreneurial decision-making: examining preferences for causal and effectual logics in the early stage of new ventures. *Small Business Economics, 36*(3), 281–298.

Gazzaley, A., & Rosen, L. D. (2016). *The Distracted Mind: Ancient Brains in a High-Tech World*. Cambridge: MIT Press.

Gigerenzer, G. (1991). From tools to theories: A heuristic of discovery in cognitive psychology. *Psychological Review, 98*(2), 254.

Gigerenzer, G. (2018). The bias bias in behavioral economics. *Review of Behavioral Economics, 5*(3–4), 303–336.

Gollinger, T. L., & Morgan, J. B. (1993). Calculation of an efficient frontier for a commercial loan portfolio. *Journal of Portfolio Management, 19*(2), 39.

Gompers, P., Kovner, A., Lerner, J., & Scharfstein, D. S. (2006). *Skill vs. luck in entrepreneurship and venture capital: Evidence from serial entrepreneurs*. National Bureau of Economic Research: Cambridge, MA.

Goodman, N. (1983). *Fact, Fiction and Forecast*. Cambridge, MA: Harvard University Press.

Goodman, R. (2021). William James. Winter 2021. https://plato.stanford.edu/archives/win2021/entries/james/

Gopnik, A., & Wellman, H. M. (1992). Why the child's theory of mind really is a theory. *Mind b Language, 7*(1&2), 145–171.

Gould, S. J., & Vrba, E. S. (1982). Exaptation – a missing term in the science of form. *Paleobiology, 8*(1), 4–15.

Grimes, M. G. (2018). The pivot: How founders respond to feedback through idea and identity work. *Academy of Management Journal, 61*(5), 1692–1717.

Hambrick, D. Z., Burgoyne, A. P., Macnamara, B. N., & Ullén, F. (2018). Toward a multifactorial model of expertise: Beyond born versus made. *Annals of the New York Academy of Sciences, 1423*(1), 284–295.

Hardin, G. (1968). The tragedy of the commons. *Science 162*, 1243–1248.

Harms, R., & Schiele, H. (2012). Antecedents and consequences of effectuation and causation in the international new venture creation process. *Journal of International Entrepreneurship, 10*(2), 95–116.

Harris, L., Lee, V. K., Thompson, E. H., & Kranton, R. (2016). Exploring the generalization process from past behavior to predicting future behavior. *Journal of Behavioral Decision Making, 29*(4), 419–436.

Hastie, R. (2001). Problems for judgment and decision making. *Annual Review of Psychology, 52*(1), 653–683.

Hayek, F. A. (1984). Competition as a discovery procedure. In C. Nishiyama, & K. Leube (Eds.), *The Essence of Hayek* (pp. 257). Stanford: Stanford University Press.

Hayward, M. L., Forster, W. R., Sarasvathy, S. D., & Fredrickson, B. L. (2010). Beyond hubris: How highly confident entrepreneurs rebound to venture again. *Journal of Business Venturing, 25*(6), 569–578.

Headd, B. (2003). Redefining business success: Distinguishing between closure and failure. *Small Business Economics, 21*, 51–61.

Hébert, R. F., & Link, A. N. (2007). Historical perspectives on the entrepreneur. *Foundations and Trends® in Entrepreneurship, 2*(4), 261–408.

Hechter, M., & Kanazawa, S. (1997). Sociological rational choice theory. *Annual Review of Sociology, 23*(1), 191–214.

Hindman, M. (2015). Building better models: Prediction, replication, and machine learning in the social sciences. *The Annals of the American Academy of Political and Social Science, 659*(1), 48–62.

Holland, D. V., & Shepherd, D. A. (2013). Deciding to persist: Adversity, values, and entrepreneurs' decision policies. *Entrepreneurship Theory and Practice, 37*(2), 331–358.

Huang, L., & Knight, A. P. (2017). Resources and relationships in entrepreneurship: An exchange theory of the development and effects of the entrepreneur-investor relationship. *Academy of Management Review, 42*(1), 80–102.

Hunt, L. (2007). *Inventing Human Rights: A History*. WW Norton.

Joas, H. (1996). *The Creativity of Action*. Chicago: University of Chicago Press.

Kahneman, D., & Tversky, A. (1979). Prospect theory: An analysis of decision under risk. *Econometrica, 47*(2), 363–391.

Kamat, M. A., Blackshaw, J. A., Young, R., et al. (2019). PhenoScanner V2: An expanded tool for searching human genotype – phenotype associations. *Bioinformatics, 35*(22), 4851–4853.

Karami, M., Wooliscroft, B., & McNeill, L. (2020). Effectuation and internationalisation: A review and agenda for future research. *Small Business Economics, 55*, 777–811.

Karlson, B., Bellavitis, C., & France, N. (2021). Commercializing LanzaTech, from waste to fuel: An effectuation case. *Journal of Management & Organization, 27*(1), 175–196.

Keller, E. F. (2010). Goodbye nature vs nurture debate. *New Scientist, 207* (2778), 28–29.

Kelley, H. H. (2000). The proper study of social psychology. *Social Psychology Quarterly, 63*(1), 3–15.

Kerr, J., & Coviello, N. (2019). Formation and constitution of effectual networks: A systematic review and synthesis. *International Journal of Management Reviews, 21*(3), 370–397.

Klein, P. G. (2008). Opportunity discovery, entrepreneurial action, and economic organization. *Strategic Entrepreneurship Journal, 2*(3), 175–190.

Knight, F. H. (1921). *Risk, Uncertainty and Profit.* New York: Houghton Mifflin.

Knudsen, T. (2003). Simon's election theory: Why docility evolves to breed successful altruism. *Journal of Economic Psychology, 24*, 229–244. https://doi.org/10.1016/S0167-4870(02)00205-2

Koehn, N. F. (2001). *Brand New : How Entrepreneurs Earned Consumers' Trust from Wedgwood to Dell.* Boston, MA: Harvard Business School Press.

Koellinger, P., Minniti, M., & Schade, C. (2007). "I think I can, I think I can": Overconfidence and entrepreneurial behavior. *Journal of Economic Psychology, 28*(4), 502–527.

Kuusela, H., & Paul, P. (2000). A comparison of concurrent and retrospective verbal protocol analysis. *American Journal of Psychology, 113*(3), 387–404.

Langer, E. (2005). Well-being: Mindfulness versus positive evaluation. In C. R. Snyder & S. J. Lopez (Eds.), *Handbook of Positive Psychology*, (pp. 214–230). New York: Oxford University Press.

Lawless, R. M., & Warren, E. (2005). The myth of the disappearing business bankruptcy. *California Law Review, 93*, 743.

Leca, B., Battilana, J., & Boxenbaum, E. (2008). *Agency and Institutions: A Review of Institutional Entrepreneurship*, (pp. 8–96). Cambridge, MA: Harvard Business School .

Levi-Strauss, C. (1966). *The Savage Mind.* Chicago, IL: University of Chicago Press.

Liedtka, J. (2014). Innovative ways companies are using design thinking. *Strategy & Leadership.*

Lillard, A. S., & Erisir, A. (2011). Old dogs learning new tricks: Neuroplasticity beyond the juvenile period. *Developmental review, 31*(4), 207–239.

Loasby, B. J. (1999). *Knowledge, Institutions and Evolution in Economics.* London: Routledge.

Loasby, B. J. (2001). Time, knowledge and evolutionary dynamics: Why Connections Matter. *Journal of Evolutionary Economics*, *11*(4), 393–412.

Luzzi, A., & Sasson, A. (2016). Individual entrepreneurial exit and earnings in subsequent paid employment. *Entrepreneurship Theory and Practice*, *40*(2), 401–420.

MacCrimmon, K. R., & Wehrung, D. A. (1990). Characteristics of risk taking executives. *Management Science*, *36*(4), 422–435.

Mainela, T., & Puhakka, V. (2009). Organising new business in a turbulent context: Opportunity discovery and effectuation for IJV development in transition markets. *Journal of International Entrepreneurship*, *7*(2), 111–134.

Makadok, R., & Walker, G. (1996). Search and selection in the money market fund industry. *Strategic Management Journal*, *17*(S1), 39–54.

March, J. G. (1978). Bounded rationality, ambiguity, and the engineering of choice. *Bell Journal of Economics*, *9*(2), 587–608.

March, J. G., & Shapira, Z. (1987). Managerial perspectives on risk and risk taking. *Management Science*, *33*(11), 1404–1418.

Markowitz, H. M. (1991). Foundations of portfolio theory. *The Journal of Finance*, *46*(2), 469–477.

Marshall, A. (1890 [2009]). *Principles of Economics: Unabridged, 8th ed.* New York: Cosimo.

Martina, R. A. (2018). Toward a theory of affordable loss. *Small Business Economics*, *54*(3), 751–774.

Marx, K. (1867). *Capital: A Critique of Political economy. Volume 1, Part 1: The Process of Capitalist Production*. New York: Cosimo.

Mazzucato, M. (2015). *Entrepreneurial State: Debunking Public vs. Private Sector Myths*. London: Anthem Press.

McAdams, D. P., & Olson, B. D. (2010). Personality development: Continuity and change over the life course. *Annual Review of Psychology*, *61*, 517–542.

McNally, D. (1993). *Against the Market: Political Economy, Market Socialism and the Marxist Critique*. London: Verso.

Mirowski, P. (1991). *More Heat than Light: Economics as Social Physics, Physics as Nature's Economics*. Cambridge: Cambridge University Press.

Molden, D. C., & Dweck, C. S. (2006). Finding "meaning" in psychology: A lay theories approach to self-regulation, social perception, and social development. *American Psychologist*, *61*(3), 192.

Mooradian, T., Matzler, K., Uzelac, B., & Bauer, F. (2016). Perspiration and inspiration: Grit and innovativeness as antecedents of entrepreneurial success. *Journal of Economic Psychology*, *56*, 232–243.

Moses, L. B. (2007). Recurring dilemmas: The law's race to keep up with technological change. *University of Illinois Journal of Law, Technology, & Policy*, 2007 (2), 239.

Moyo, D. (2009). *Dead Aid: Why Aid Is Not Working and How There Is a Better Way for Africa*. London: Macmillan.

Murphy, M., Danis, W. M., & Mack, J. (2020). From principles to action: Community-based entrepreneurship in the Toquaht Nation. *Journal of Business Venturing*, *35*(6), 106051.

Murphy, M. C., & Dweck, C. S. (2010). A culture of genius: How an organization's lay theory shapes people's cognition, affect, and behavior. *Personality and Social Psychology Bulletin*, *36*(3), 283–296.

Nahata, R. (2019). Success is good but failure is not so bad either: Serial entrepreneurs and venture capital contracting. *Journal of Corporate Finance*, *58*, 624–649.

Brandenburger, A. M., and Nalebuff, B. J. (1996). *Co-Opetition*. Currency/Doubleday:New York.

Nambisan, S., Siegel, D., & Kenney, M. (2018). On open innovation, platforms, and entrepreneurship. *Strategic Entrepreneurship Journal*, *12*(3), 354–368.

Nielsen, K., & Sarasvathy, S. D. (2016). A market for lemons in serial entrepreneurship? Exploring type I and type II errors in the restart decision. *Academy of Management Discoveries*, *2*(3), 247–271.

Nielsen, K., & Sarasvathy, S. D. (2018). Exit perspective on entrepreneurship. In Turcan, R. and Fraser, N. (Eds.), *The Palgrave Handbook of Multidisciplinary Perspectives on Entrepreneurship* (pp. 223–245). Springer.

OECD. (2015). High-growth enterprises rate. In *Entrepreneurship at a Glance*. Paris: OECD.

OECD. (2016). Survival of enterprises. In *Entrepreneurship at a Glance*. Paris: OECD.

Olive-Tomas, A., & Harmeling, S. S. (2020). The rise of art movements: An effectual process model of Picasso's and Braque's give-and-take during the creation of Cubism (1908–1914). *Small Business Economics*, *54*(3), 819–842.

Olson Jr., M. (1971). *The Logic of Collective Action: Public Goods and the Theory of Groups, with a new preface and appendix* (Vol. 124), Cambridge MA: Harvard University Press.

Ostrom, E. (2010). Beyond markets and states: Polycentric governance of complex economic systems. *American Economic Review*, *100*(3), 641–672.

Pareto, V., Schwier, A. S., & Page, A. N. (1971). *Manual of Political Economy*. London: Macmillan.

Parker, S. C. (2013). Do serial entrepreneurs run successively better-performing businesses? *Journal of Business Venturing, 28*(5), 652–666.

Pearl, J. (2009). *Causality*. Cambridge: Cambridge university press.

Petroski, H. (1985). *To Engineer Is Human: The Role of Failure in Successful Design*. New York: St Martins Press.

Plag, I. (2006). Productivity. In Bas Aarts & April M. McMahon (Eds.), *The handbook of English linguistics*, (pp. 483–499). Oxford: Blackwell.

Penrose, E. (1959). *The Theory of the Growth of the Firm*. New York: Oxford University Press.

Pfeffer, J., & Salancik, G. R. (1978). *The External Control of Organizations: A Resource Dependence Perspective*. New York: Harper & Row.

Poschke, M. (2013). "Entrepreneurs out of necessity": A snapshot. *Applied Economics Letters, 20*(7), 658–663.

Porter, M. E. (2008). The five competitive forces that shape strategy. *Harvard Business Review, 86*(1), 78.

Posen, H. E., Keil, T., Kim, S., & Meissner, F. D. (2018). Renewing research on problemistic search – A review and research agenda. *Academy of Management Annals, 12*(1), 208–251.

Read, S., Dew, N., Sarasvathy, S. D., Song, M., & Wiltbank, R. (2009). Marketing under uncertainty: The logic of an effectual approach. *Journal of Marketing, 73*(3), 1–18.

Read, S., Sarasvathy, S., Dew, N., & Wiltbank, R. (2016). *Effectual Entrepreneurship*. Abingdon: Routledge.

Read, S., Song, M., & Smit, W. (2009). A meta-analytic review of effectuation and venture performance. *Journal of Business Venturing, 24*(6), 573–587.

Reymen, I., Berends, H., Oudehand, R., & Stultiëns, R. (2017). Decision making for business model development: A process study of effectuation and causation in new technology-based ventures. *R&D Management, 47*(4), 595–606.

Roberts, R. M. (1989). *Serendipity: Accidental Discoveries in Science*. New York: Wiley.

Roemer, J. E. (1988). *Free to Lose: An Introduction to Marxist Economic Philosophy* (Vol. 360). Cambridge: Harvard University Press.

Rosling, H. (2019). *Factfulness*. Flammarion. New York: Flatiron Books

Rychlak, J. F. (1964). Control and prediction and the clinician. *American Psychologist, 19*(3), 186.

Sackett, P. R., Gruys, M. L., & Ellingson, J. E. (1998). Ability – personality interactions when predicting job performance. *Journal of Applied Psychology, 83*(4), 545.

Shane, S. A. (2003). *A General Theory of Entrepreneurship: The Individual-Opportunity Nexus.* Northampton: Edward Elgar Publishing Incorporated.

Saini, A. (2018). *Picking Winners: A Big Data Approach to Evaluating Startups and Making Venture Capital Investments.* Cambridge: Massachusetts Institute of Technology.

Salgado, J. F. (2003). Predicting job performance using FFM and non-FFM personality measures. *Journal of Occupational and Organizational Psychology, 76*(3), 323–346.

Sarason, Y., Dean, T., & Dillard, J. F. (2006). Entrepreneurship as the nexus of individual and opportunity: A structuration view. *Journal of Business Venturing, 21*(3), 286–305.

Sarasvathy, S. D. (2001). Causation and effectuation: Toward a theoretical shift from economic inevitability to entrepreneurial contingency. *Academy of Management: The Academy of Management Review, 26*(2), 243–263.

Sarasvathy, D. K., Simon, H. A., & Lave, L. (1998). Perceiving and managing business risks: Differences between entrepreneurs and bankers. *Journal of Economic Behavior and Organization, 33*(2), 207–225.

Sarasvathy, S. D. (2009). *Effectuation: Elements of Entrepreneurial Expertise.* Cheltenham: Edward Elgar.

Sarasvathy, S. D. (2021). An Effectual Analysis of Markets and States. In K. Wennberg, & C. Sandström (Eds.), *Questioning the Entrepreneurial State: A Revised Perspective on States and Markets* (pp. 37–55). Berlin: Springer.

Sarasvathy, S. D., & Dew, N. (2005). New market creation as transformation. *Journal of Evolutionary Economics, 15*(5), 533–565.

Sarasvathy, S. D., Menon, A. R., & Kuechle, G. (2013). Failing firms and successful entrepreneurs: Serial entrepreneurship as a temporal portfolio. *Small Business Economics, 40*(2), 417–434.

Sarasvathy, S. D., & Ramesh, A. (2019). An effectual model of collective action for addressing sustainability challenges. *Academy of Management Perspectives, 33*(4), 405–424.

Sarasvathy, S. D., & Venkataraman, S. (2011). Entrepreneurship as method: Open questions for an entrepreneurial future. *Entrepreneurship Theory and Practice, 35*(1), 113–135.

Schumpeter, J. A. (1975[1942]). The process of creative destruction. In *Capitalism, Socialism and Democracy* (pp. 81–86). New York: Harper Torchbooks.

Scott, W. R. (2005). Institutional theory: Contributing to a theoretical research program. *Great Minds in Management: The Process of Theory Development, 37*(2), 460–484.

Sellars, R. W. (1939). Positivism in contemporary philosophic thought. *American Sociological Review, 4*(1), 26–42.

Sen, A. (1999). *Development as Freedom.* New York: Anchor Books.

Servantie, V., & Rispal, M. H. (2018). Bricolage, effectuation, and causation shifts over time in the context of social entrepreneurship. *Entrepreneurship & Regional Development, 30*(3–4), 310–335.

Shaffer, J. (2012). Neuroplasticity and positive psychology in clinical practice: A review for combined benefits. *Psychology, 3*(12), 1110.

Shah, S. K., & Tripsas, M. (2007). The accidental entrepreneur: The emergent and collective process of user entrepreneurship. *Strategic Entrepreneurship Journal, 1*(1–2), 123–140.

Simon, H. A. (1964). On the concept of organizational goal. *Administrative Science Quarterly, 9*(1), 1–22.

Simon, H. A. (1996). *Sciences of the Artificial, 3rd ed.* Cambridge, MA: MIT Press.

Simon, H. A. (1997). *An Empirically-Based Microeconomics.* Cambridge: Cambridge University Press.

Simon, J. L. (1980). Resources, population, environment: An oversupply of false bad news. *Science, 208*(4451), 1431–1437.

Simonton, D. K. (1988). *Scientific Genius: A Psychology of Science.* Cambridge: Cambridge University Press.

Skousen, M. (2015). *The Big Three in Economics: Adam Smith, Karl Marx, and John Maynard Keynes: Adam Smith, Karl Marx, and John Maynard Keynes.* New York:.

Slovic, P. (1995). The construction of preference. *American Psychologist, 50* (5), 364–371.

Smith, A. (1978 [1766]). *Lectures on Jurisprudence.* Cambridge: Cambridge University Press.

Smith, A. (1822). *The Theory of Moral Sentiments* (Vol. 1). London: J. Richardson.

Smith, A. (1863). *An Inquiry into the Nature and Causes of the Wealth of Nations.*

Smolka, K. M., Verheul, I., Burmeister-Lamp, K., & Heugens, P. P. (2018). Get it together! Synergistic effects of causal and effectual decision – making logics on venture performance. *Entrepreneurship Theory and Practice, 42* (4), 571–604.

Spender, J. C. (2013). Herbert Alexander Simon: Philosopher of the organizational life-world. In M. Witzel, & M. Warner (Eds.), *The Oxford Handbook of Management Theorists* (pp. 297–358). Oxford: Oxford University Press.

Stevenson, H. H., & Jarillo, J. C. (1990). A paradigm of entrepreneurship: Entrepreneurial management. *Strategic Management Journal, 11*, 17–27.

Stigler, G. J., & Becker, G. S. (1977). De gustibus non est disputandum. *The American Economic Review, 67*(2), 76–90.

Sumner, L. (1987). *The Moral Foundation of Rights*. New York: Oxford University Press.

Szambelan, S. M., & Jiang, Y. D. (2020). Effectual control orientation and innovation performance: Clarifying implications in the corporate context. *Small Business Economics, 54*(3), 865–882.

Taleb, N. N. (2007). *The Black Swan: The Impact of the Highly Improbable*. New York, NY: Random House.

Tetlock, P. E. (2009). *Expert Political Judgment*. Princeton: Princeton University Press.

Van den Steen, E. (2004). Rational overoptimism (and other biases). *American Economic Review, 94*(4), 1141–1151.

Varian, H. R. (2014). *Intermediate Microeconomics: A Modern Approach: Ninth International, Student Edition*. New York: WW Norton.

Varzi, A. (2019). Mereology. In E. N. Zalta (Ed.), *The Stanford Encyclopedia of Philosophy* (Vol. Spring 2019). https://plato.stanford.edu/archives/win2021/entries/well-being/

Volti, R. (2005). *Society and Technological Change*. London: Macmillan.

Wasserman, N. (2003). Founder-CEO succession and the paradox of entrepreneurial success. *Organization Science, 14*(2), 149–172.

Wasserman, N. (2012). *The Founder's Dilemmas*. Princeton University Press.

Welter, F., Smallbone, D., & Pobol, A. (2015). Entrepreneurial activity in the informal economy: a missing piece of the entrepreneurship jigsaw puzzle. *Entrepreneurship & Regional Development, 27*(5–6), 292–306.

Weiss, R. (1969). *The American Myth of Success: From Horatio Alger to Norman Vincent Peale*. Chicago: University of Illinois Press.

Wennberg, K., Wiklund, J., DeTienne, D. R., & Cardon, M. S. (2010). Reconceptualizing entrepreneurial exit: Divergent exit routes and their drivers. *Journal of Business Venturing, 25*(4), 361–375.

Werndl, C. (2009). What are the new implications of chaos for unpredictability? *The British Journal for the Philosophy of Science, 60*(1), 195–220.

Westfall, R. S. (2020). The rise of science and the decline of orthodox Christianity: A study of Kepler, Descartes, and Newton. In D. C. Lindberg and R. L. Numbers (Eds.), *God and Nature* (pp. 218–237). University of California Press.

Williams, C. C., & Nadin, S. (2012). Work beyond employment: representations of informal economic activities. *Work, Employment and Society, 26*(2), 1–10.

Williamson, O. E. (1963). Managerial discretion and business behavior. *The American Economic Review, 53*(5), 1032–1057.

Williamson, O. E. (1985). *The Economic Institutions of Capitalism: Firms, Markets, Relational Contracting.* New York: Free Press.

Williamson, O. E. (1993). Opportunism and its critics. *Managerial and Decision Economics*, 14 (2), 97–107.

Wiltbank, R., Read, S., Dew, N., & Sarasvathy, S. D. (2009). Prediction and control under uncertainty: Outcomes in angel investing. *Journal of Business Venturing, 24*(2), 116–133.

Wong, P. K., Lee, L., & Der Foo, M. (2008). Occupational choice: The influence of product vs. process innovation. *Small Business Economics, 30*(3), 267–281.

Yates, J. (1992). *Risk-Taking Behavior.* New York: John Wiley.

Yin, J., & Yuan, Q. (2015). Structural homeostasis in the nervous system: A balancing act for wiring plasticity and stability. *Frontiers in Cellular Neuroscience, 8*, 439.

Cambridge Elements ☰

Business Strategy

J.-C. Spender

Kozminski University

J.-C. Spender is a research Professor, Kozminski University. He has been active in the business strategy field since 1971 and is the author or co-author of 7 books and numerous papers. His principal academic interest is in knowledge-based theories of the private sector firm, and managing them.

Advisory Board

About the Series

Business strategy's reach is vast, and important too since wherever there is business activity there is strategizing. As a field, strategy has a long history from medieval and colonial times to today's developed and developing economies. This series offers a place for interesting and illuminating research including industry and corporate studies, strategizing in service industries, the arts, the public sector, and the new forms of Internet-based commerce. It also covers today's expanding gamut of analytic techniques.

Cambridge Elements ≡

Business Strategy

Printed in the United States
by Baker & Taylor Publisher Services